Christmas

COLORING BOOK

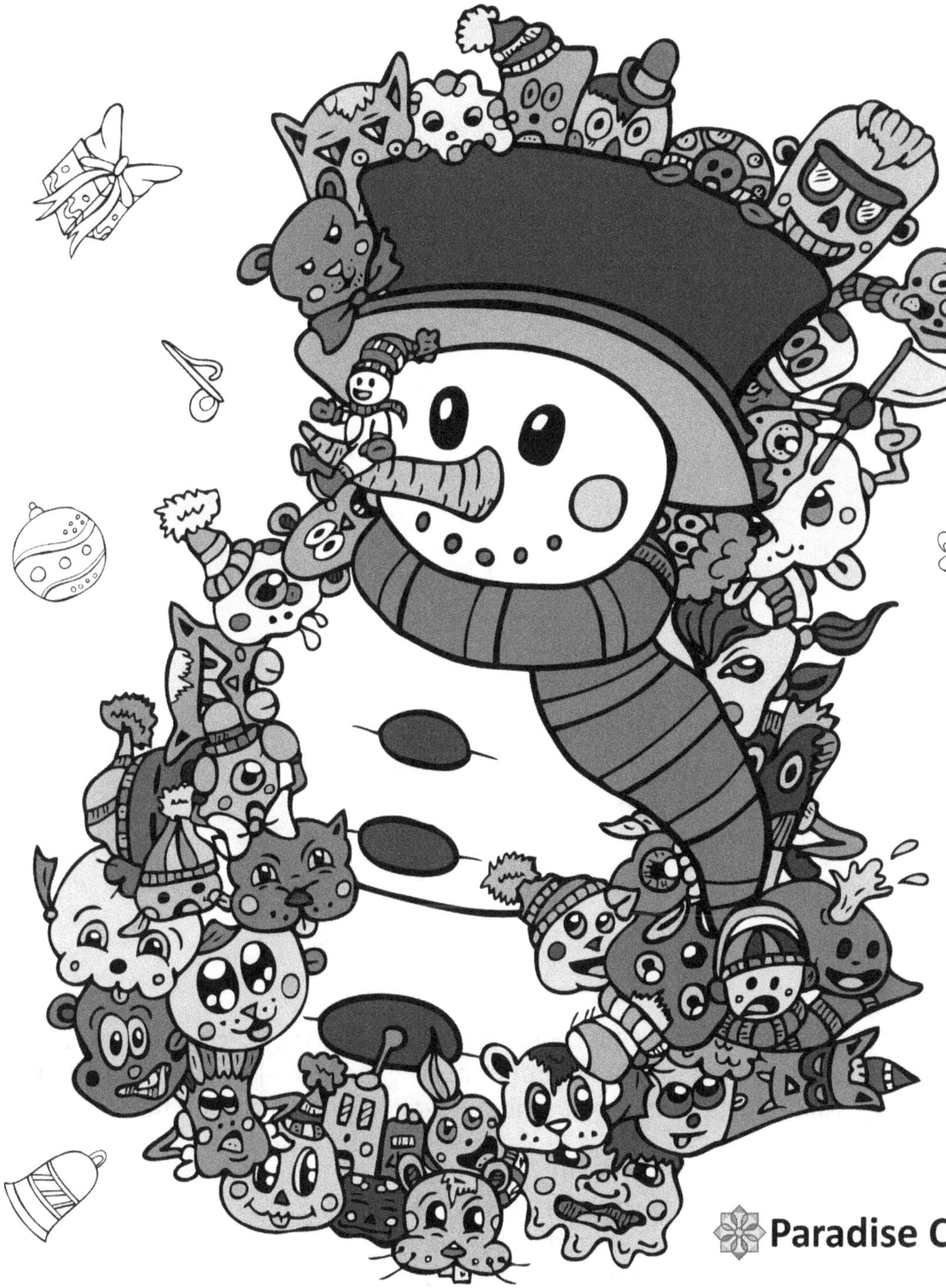

Paradise Coloring

ISBN-13: 978-1522808046
ISBN-10: 1522808043

Printed in the U.S.A.

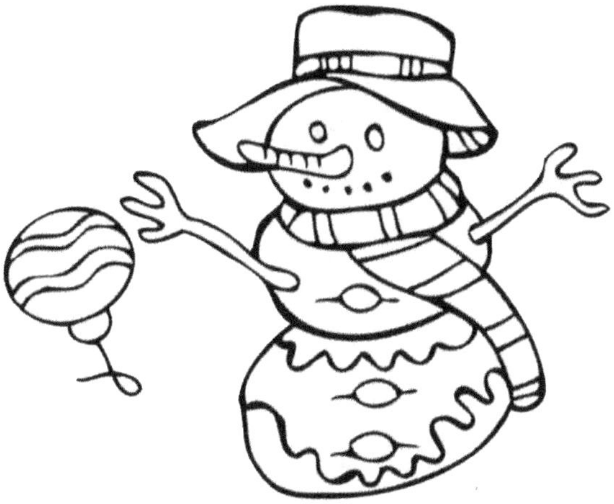

This book belongs to:

____

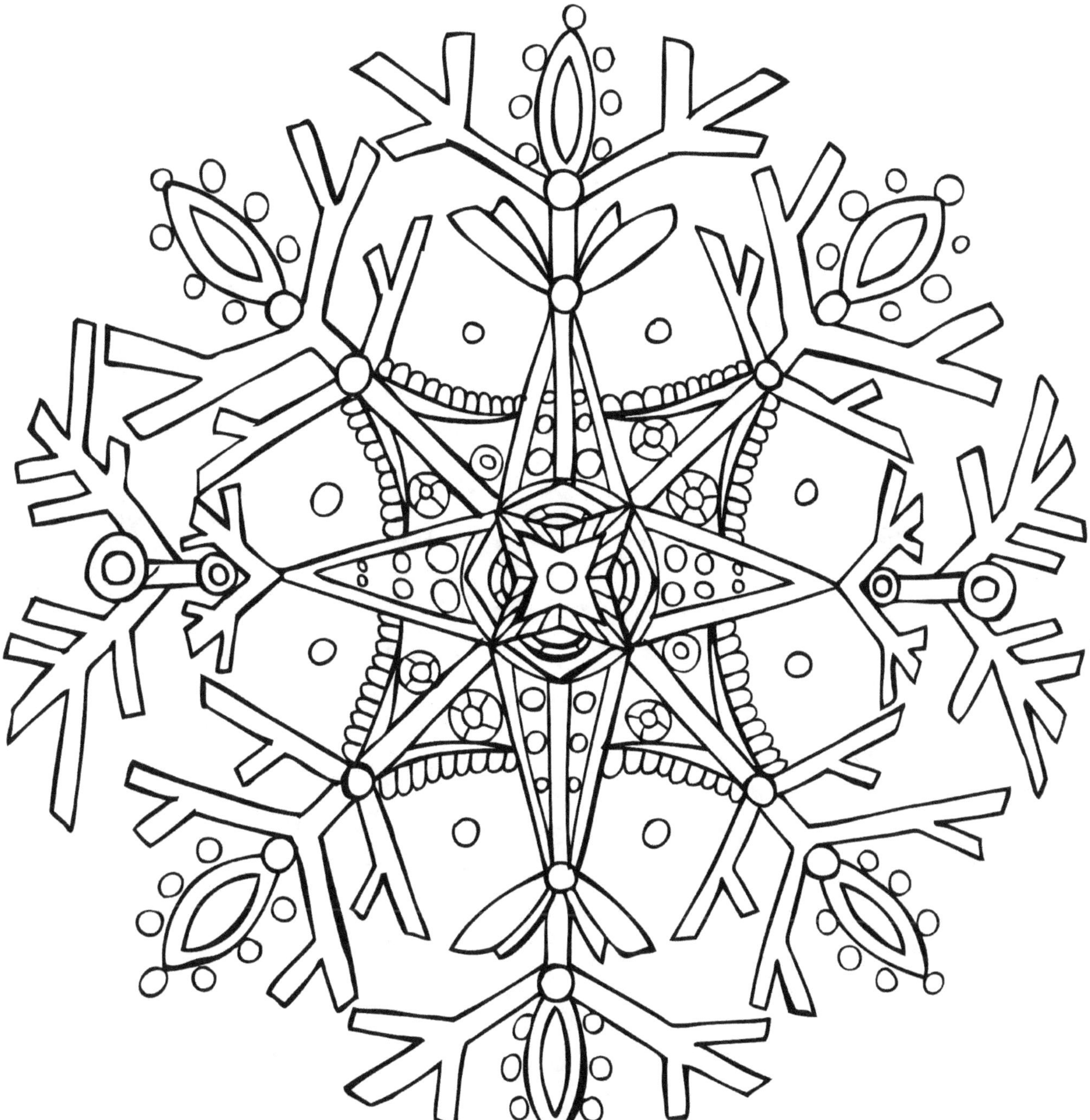

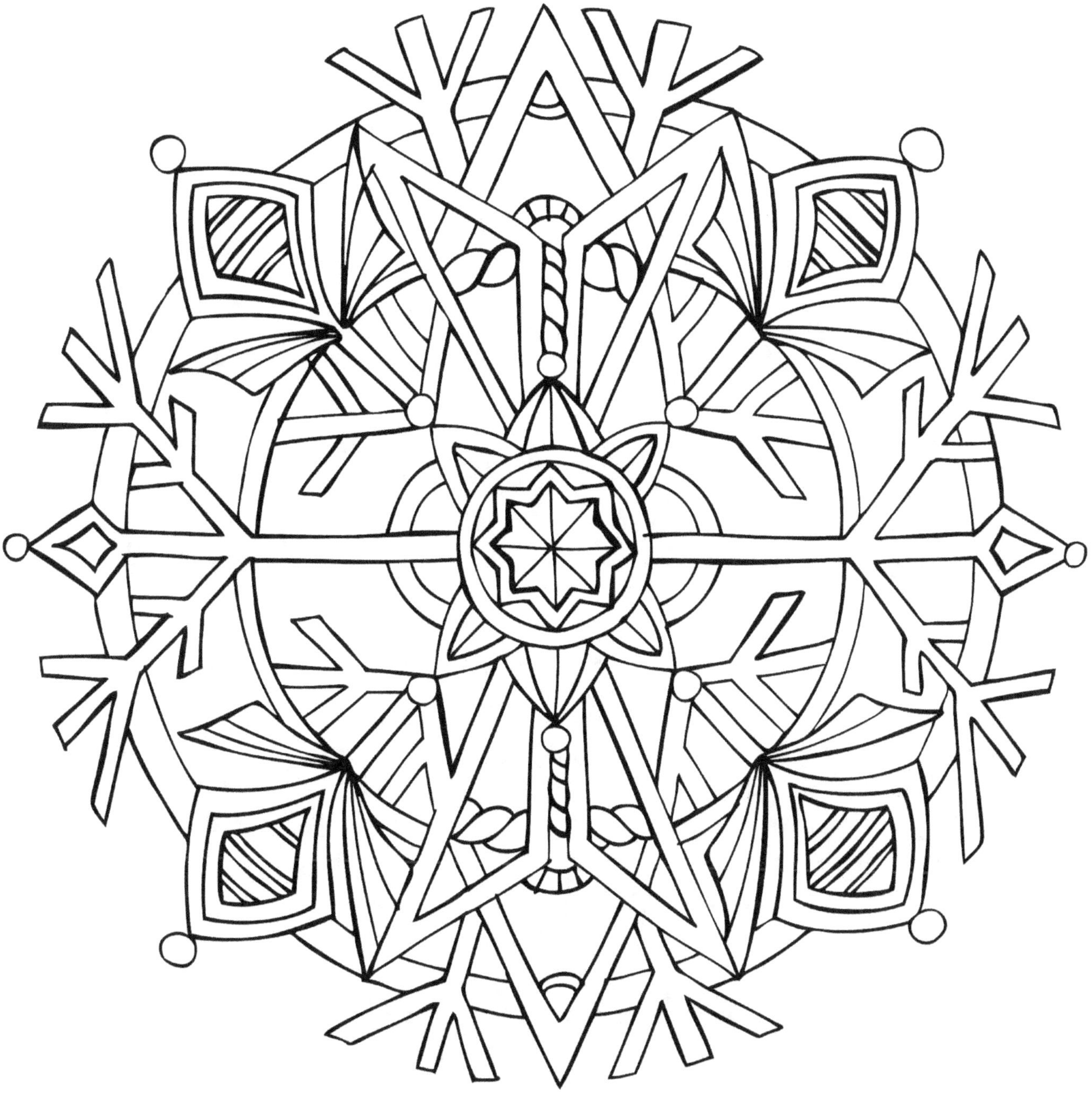

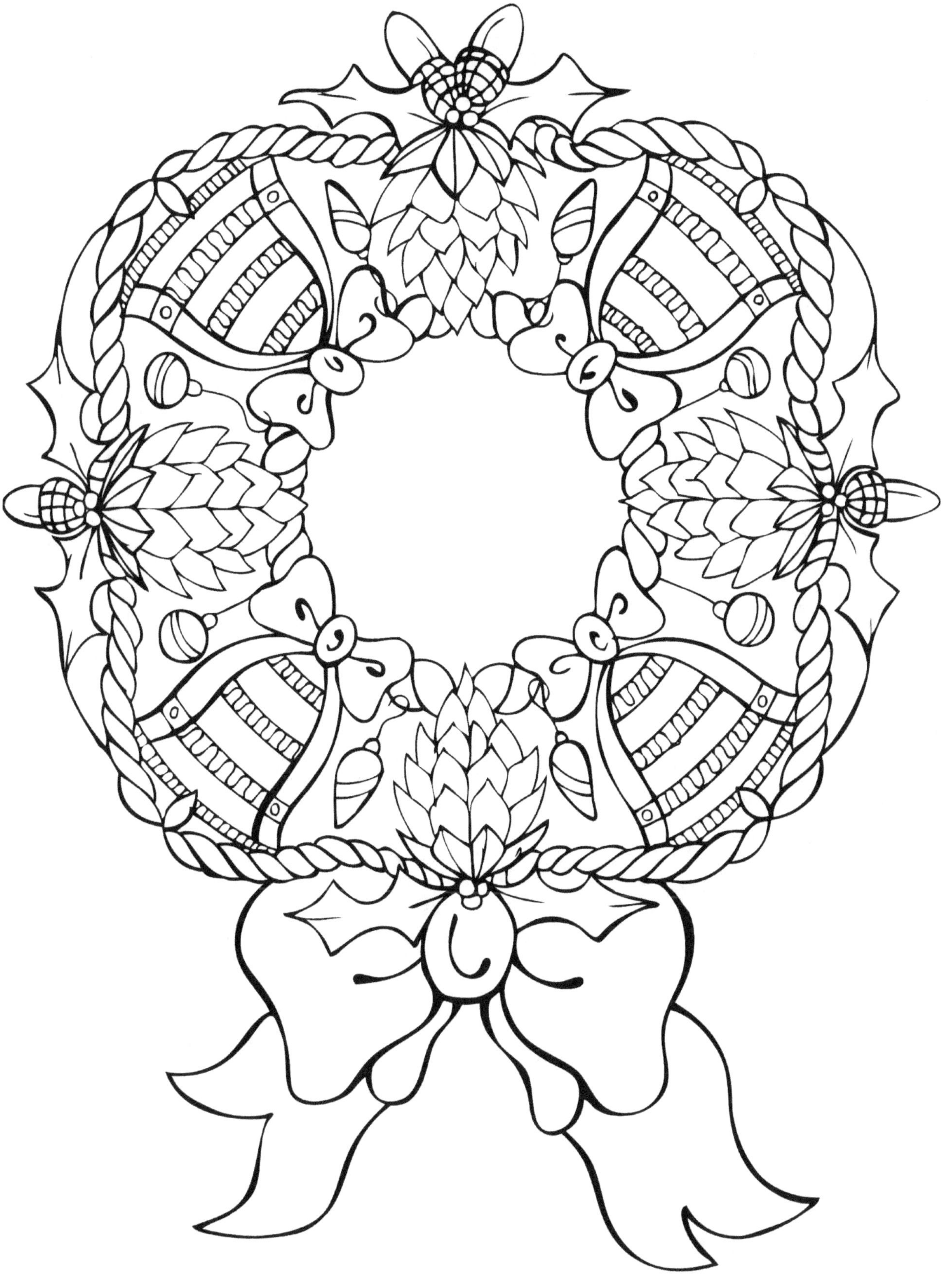

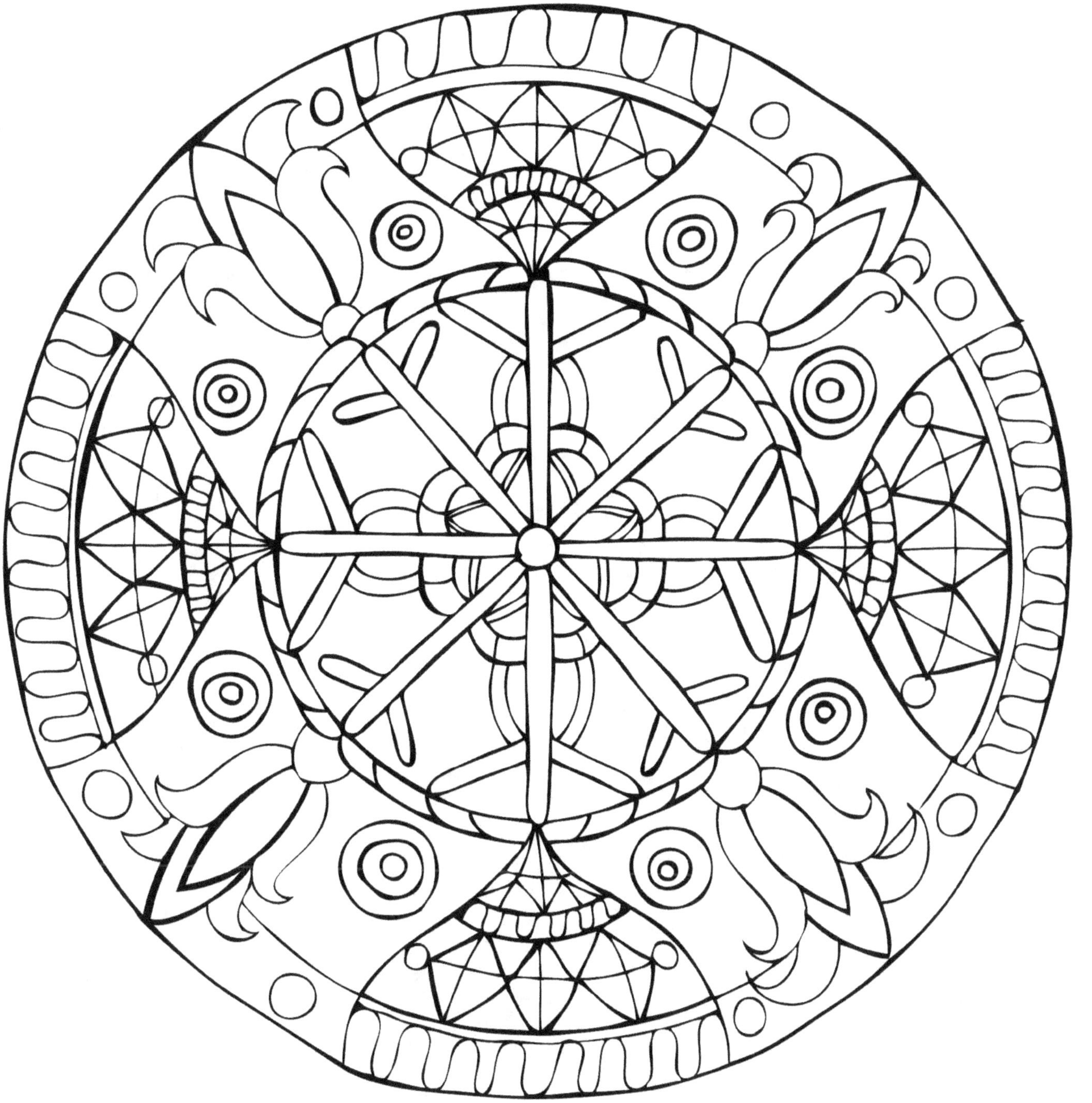

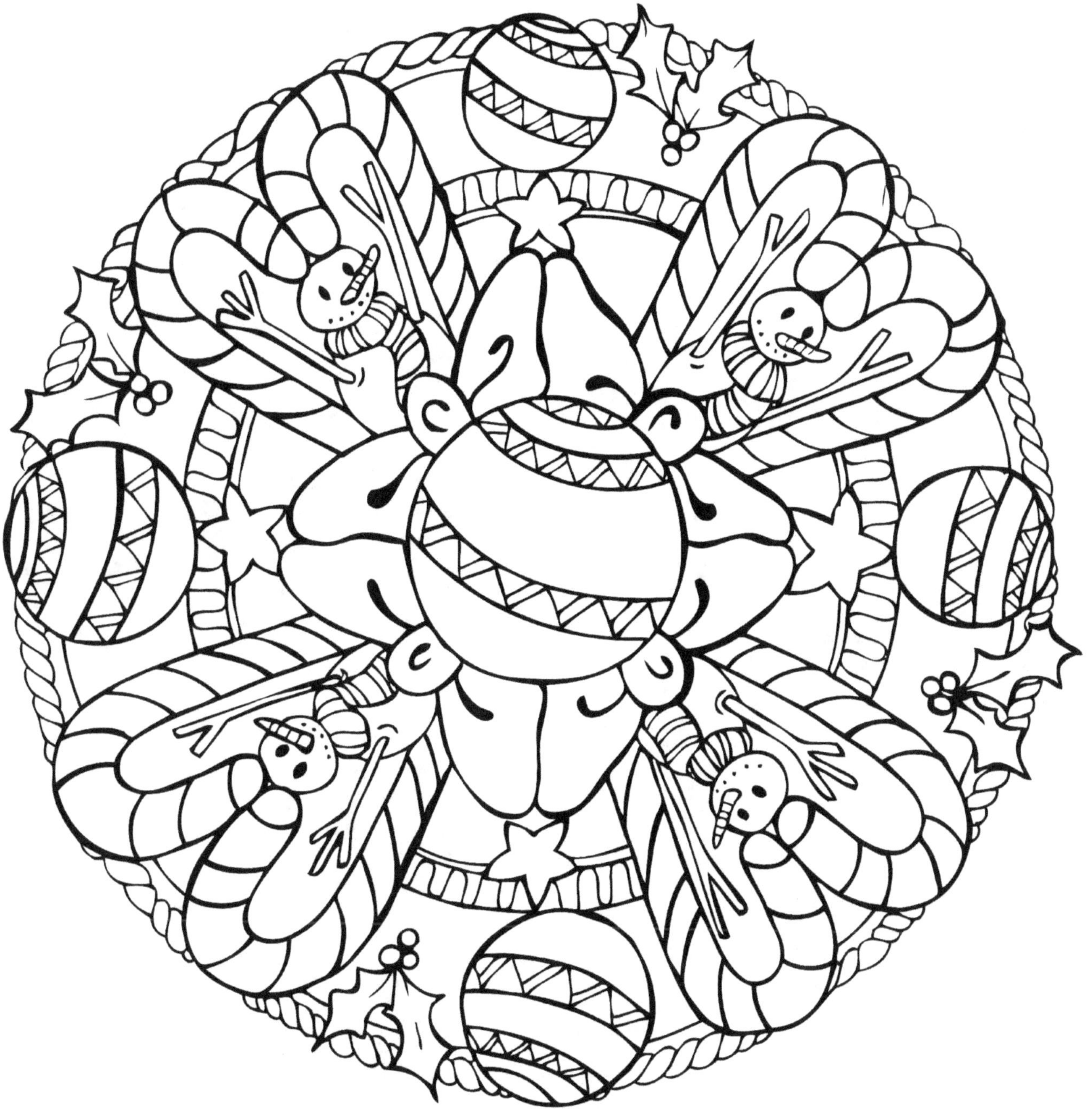

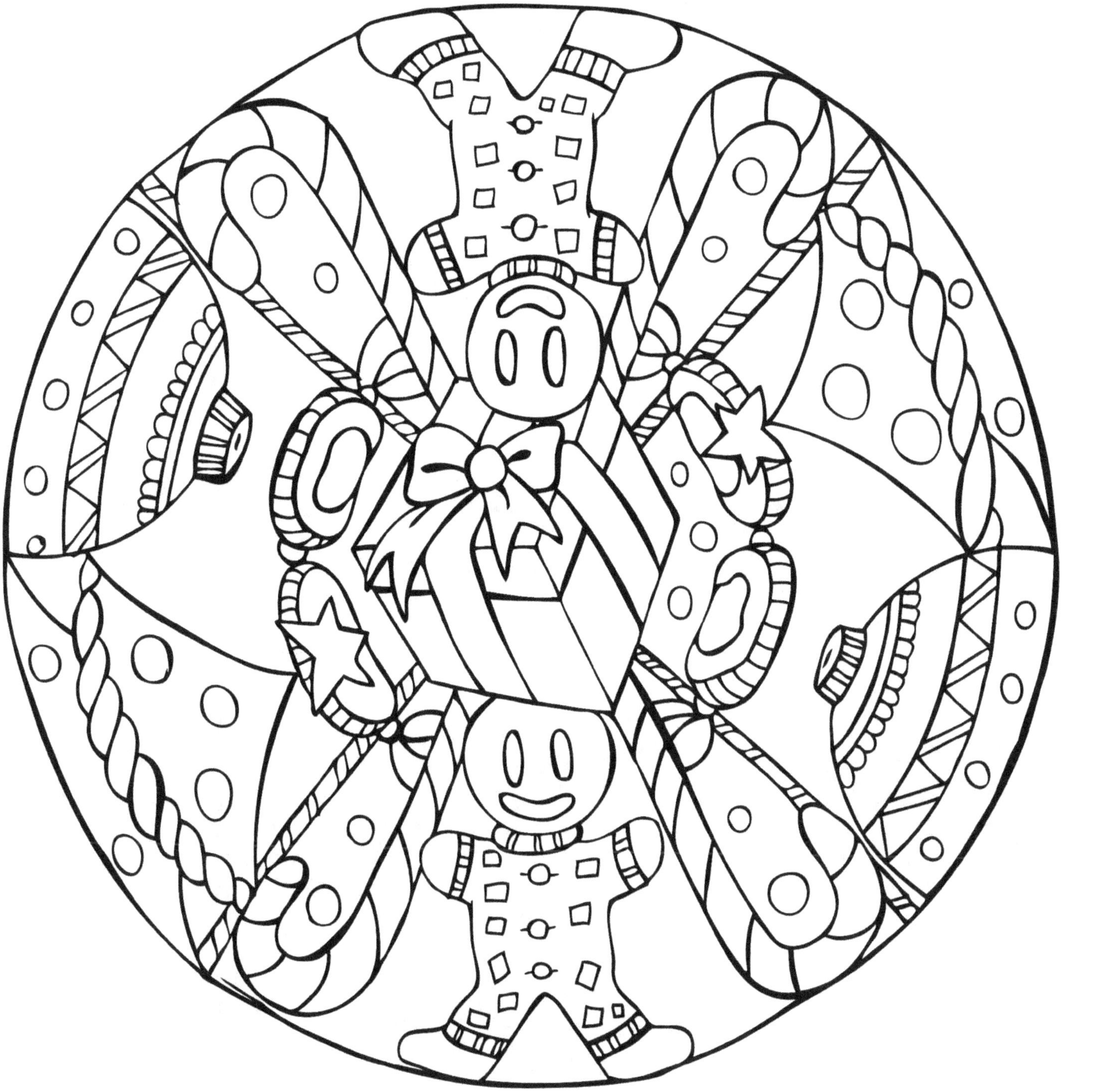

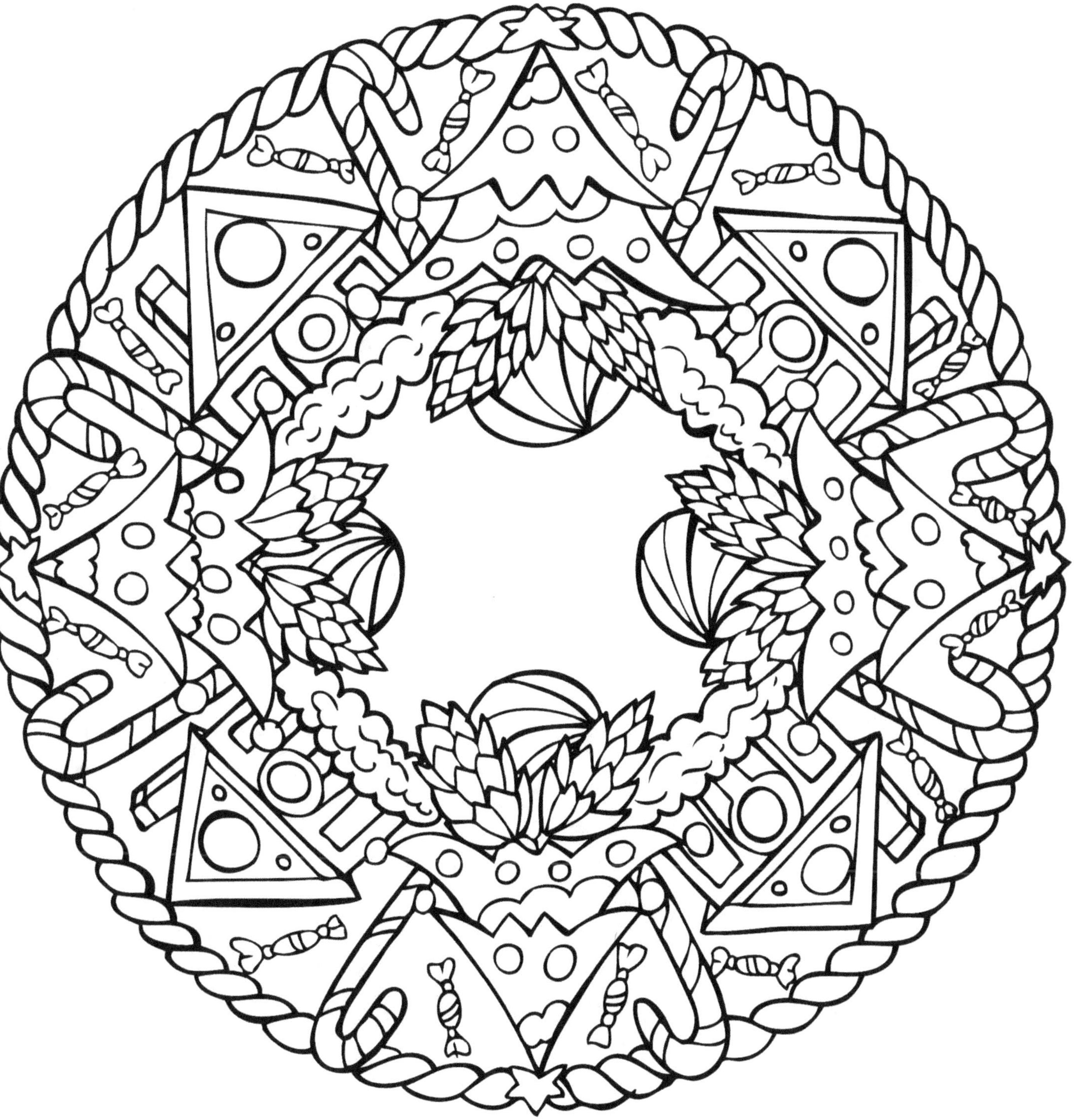

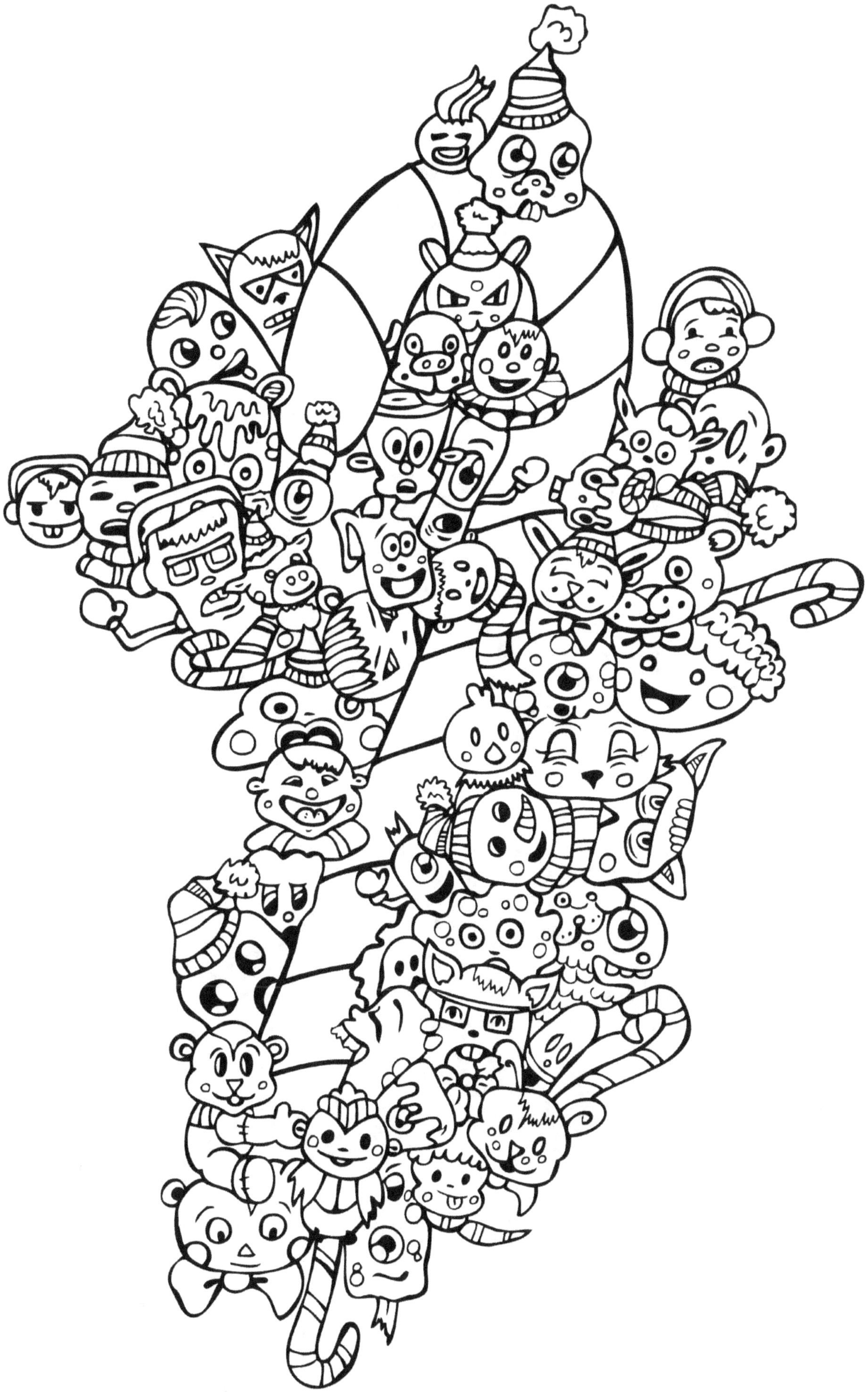

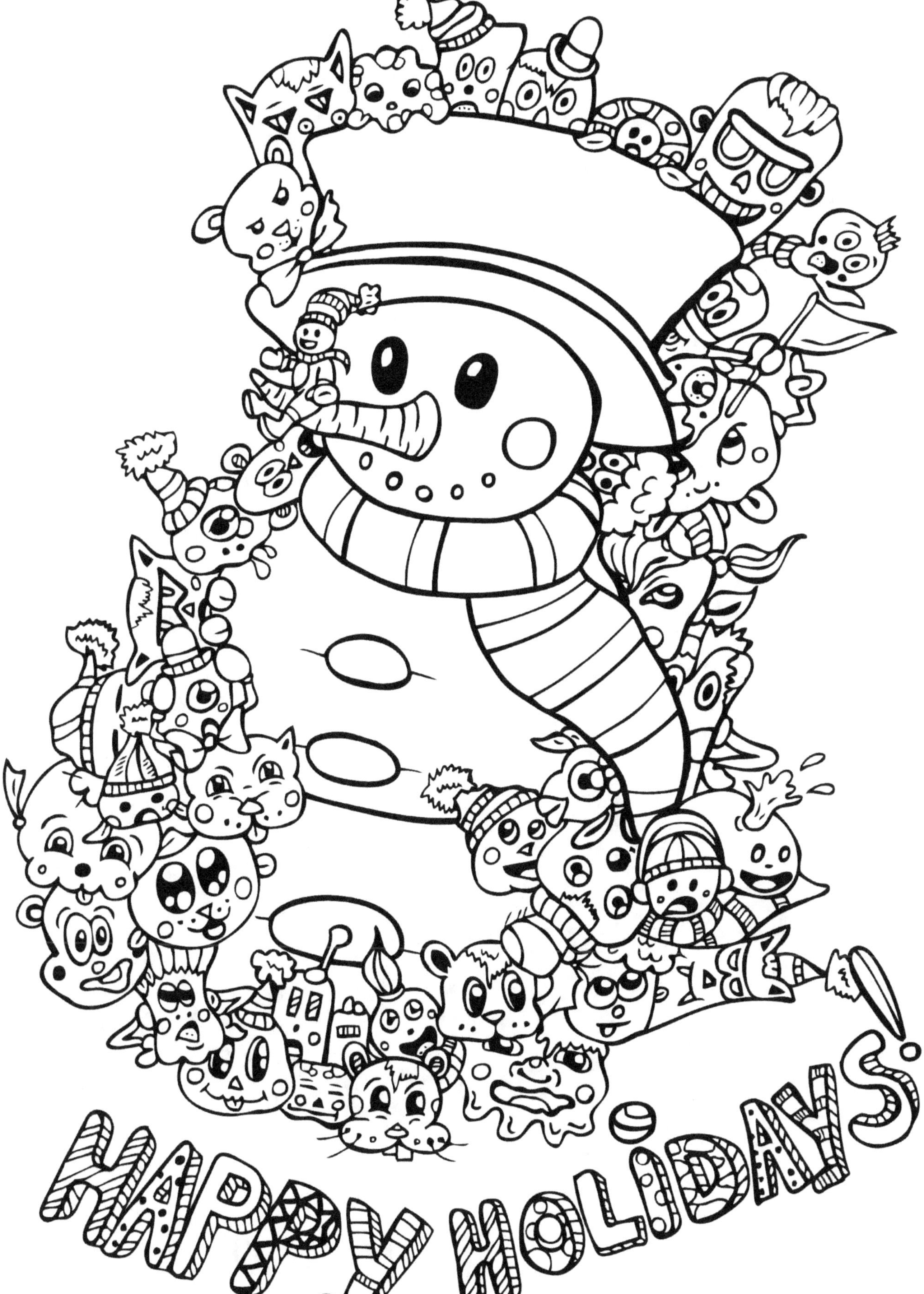
HAPPY HOLIDAYS!

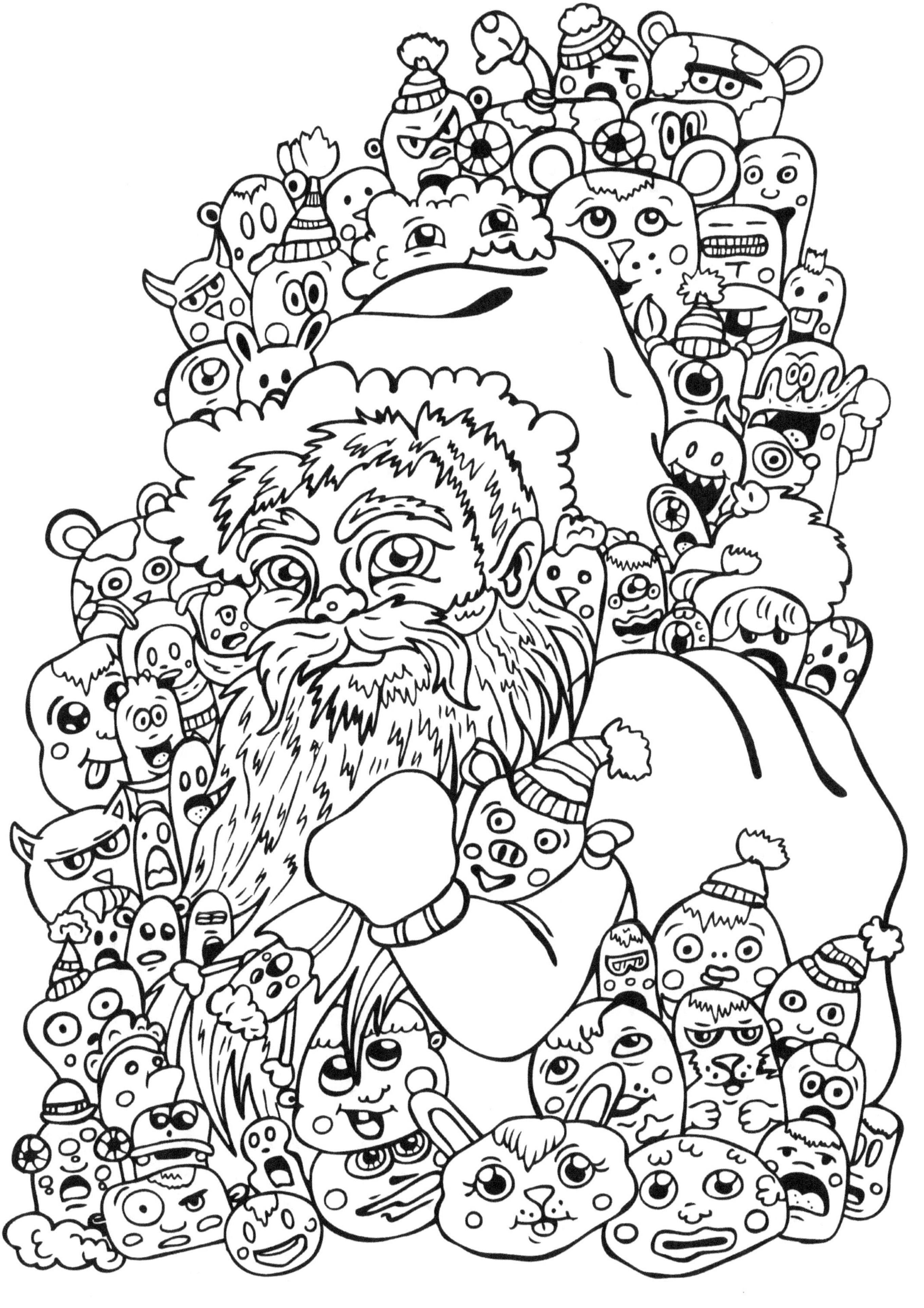

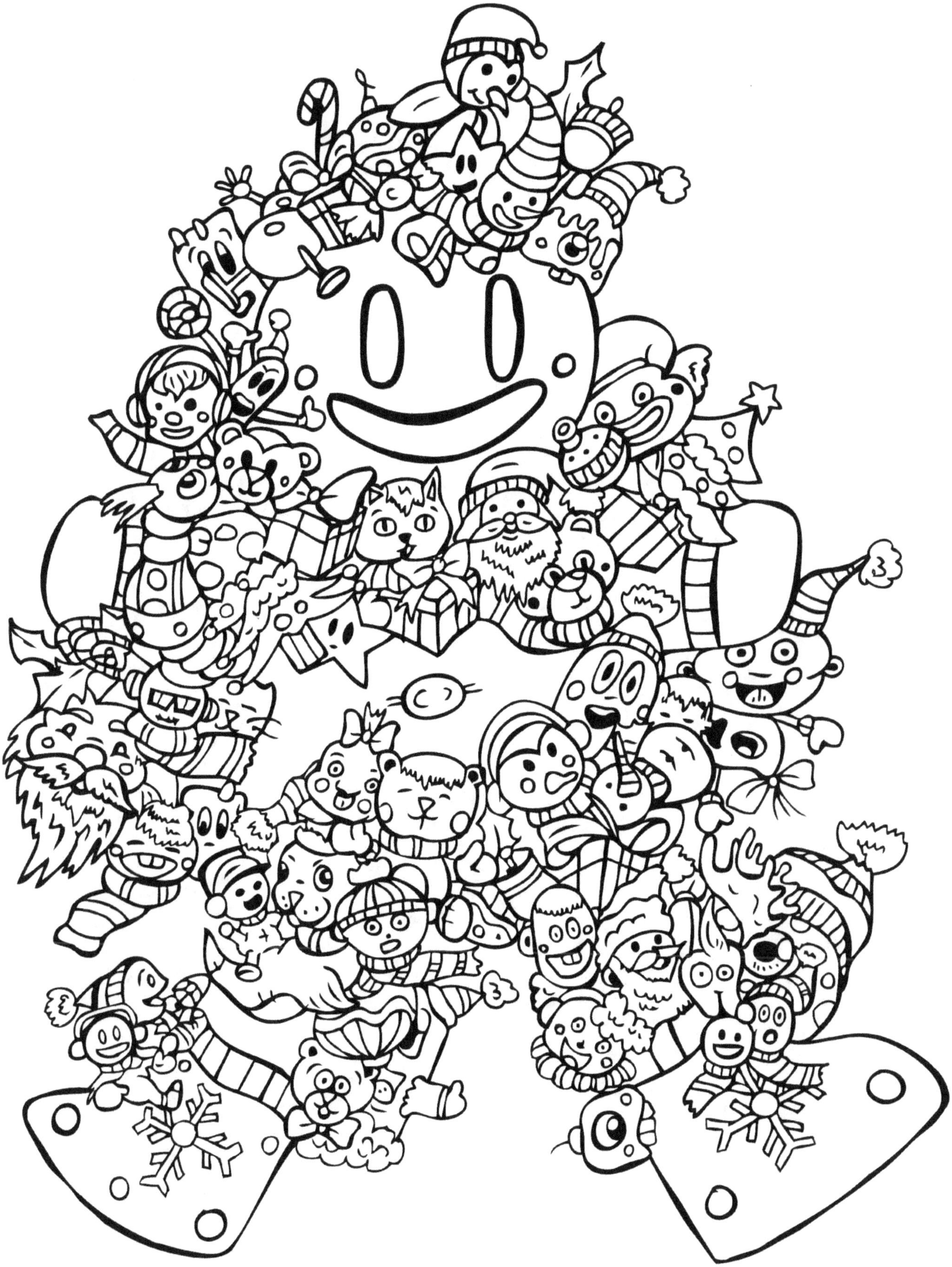

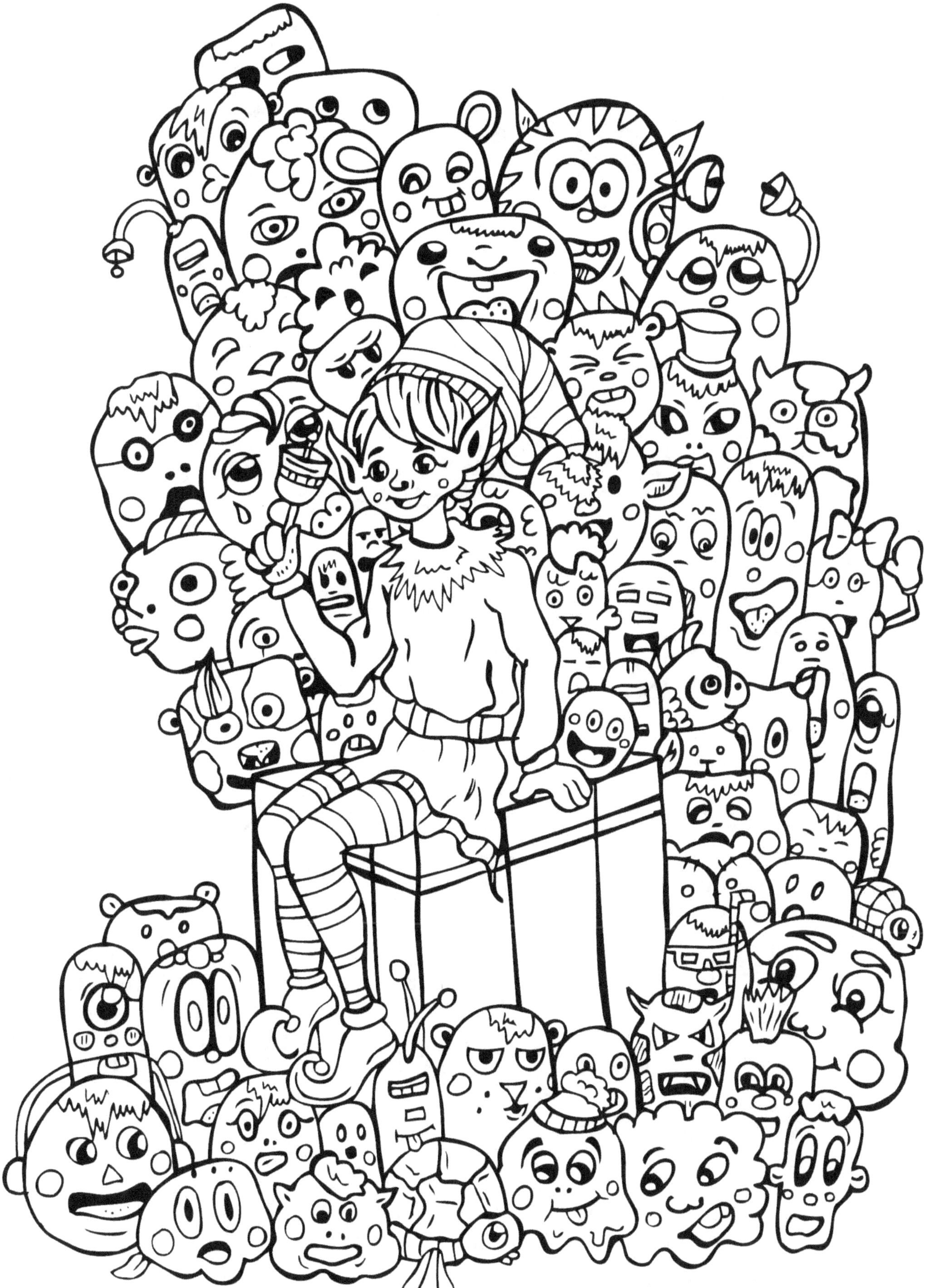

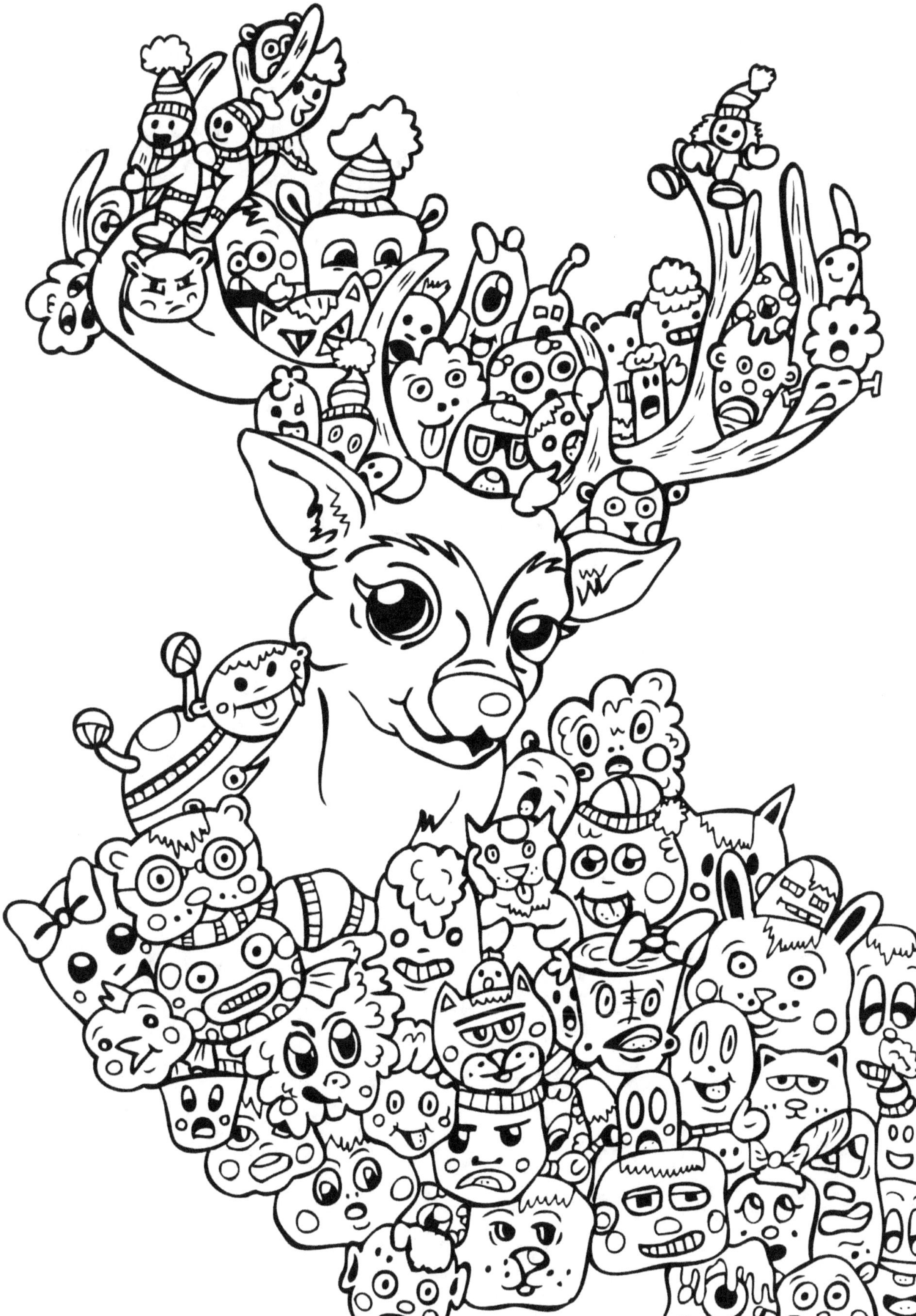

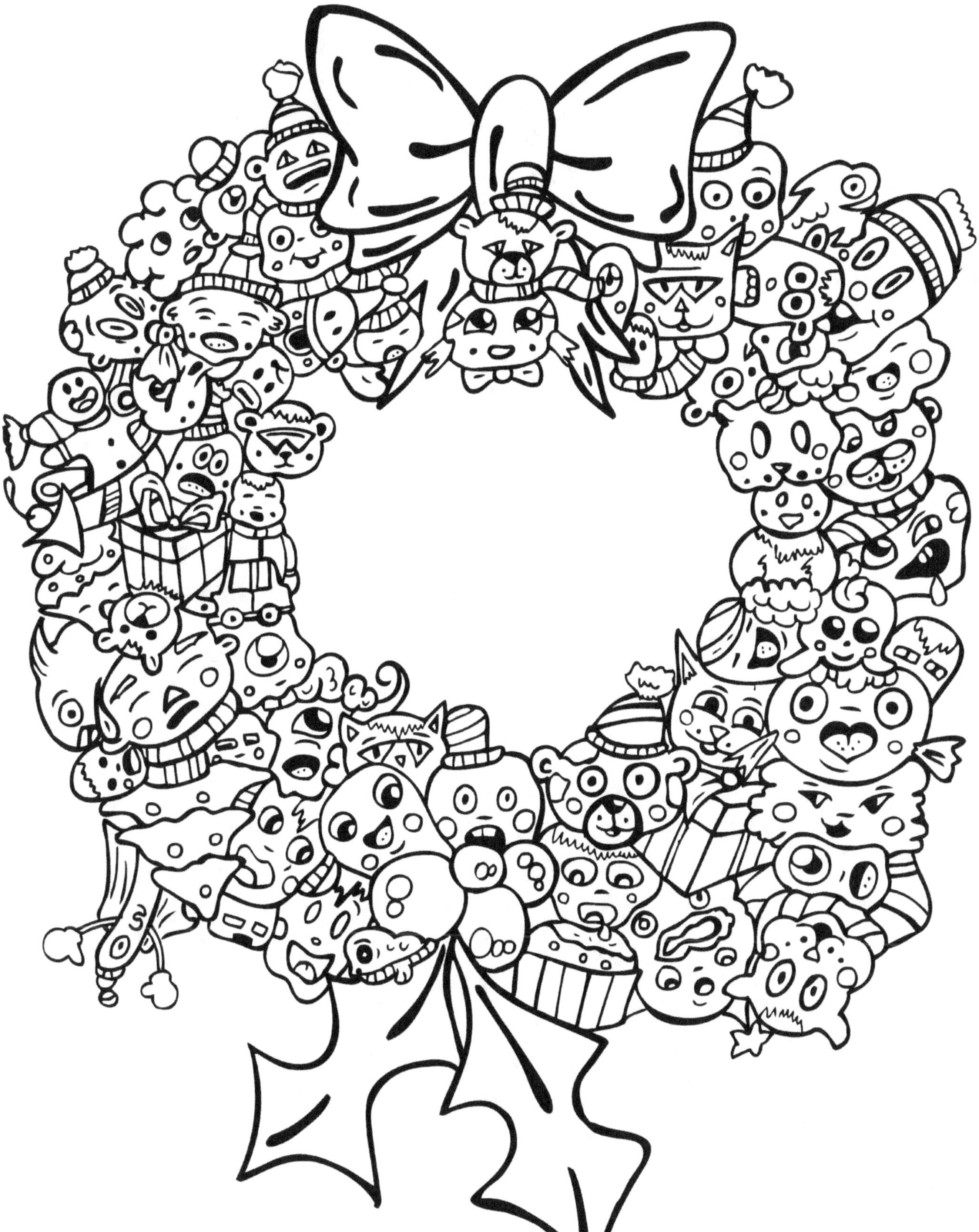

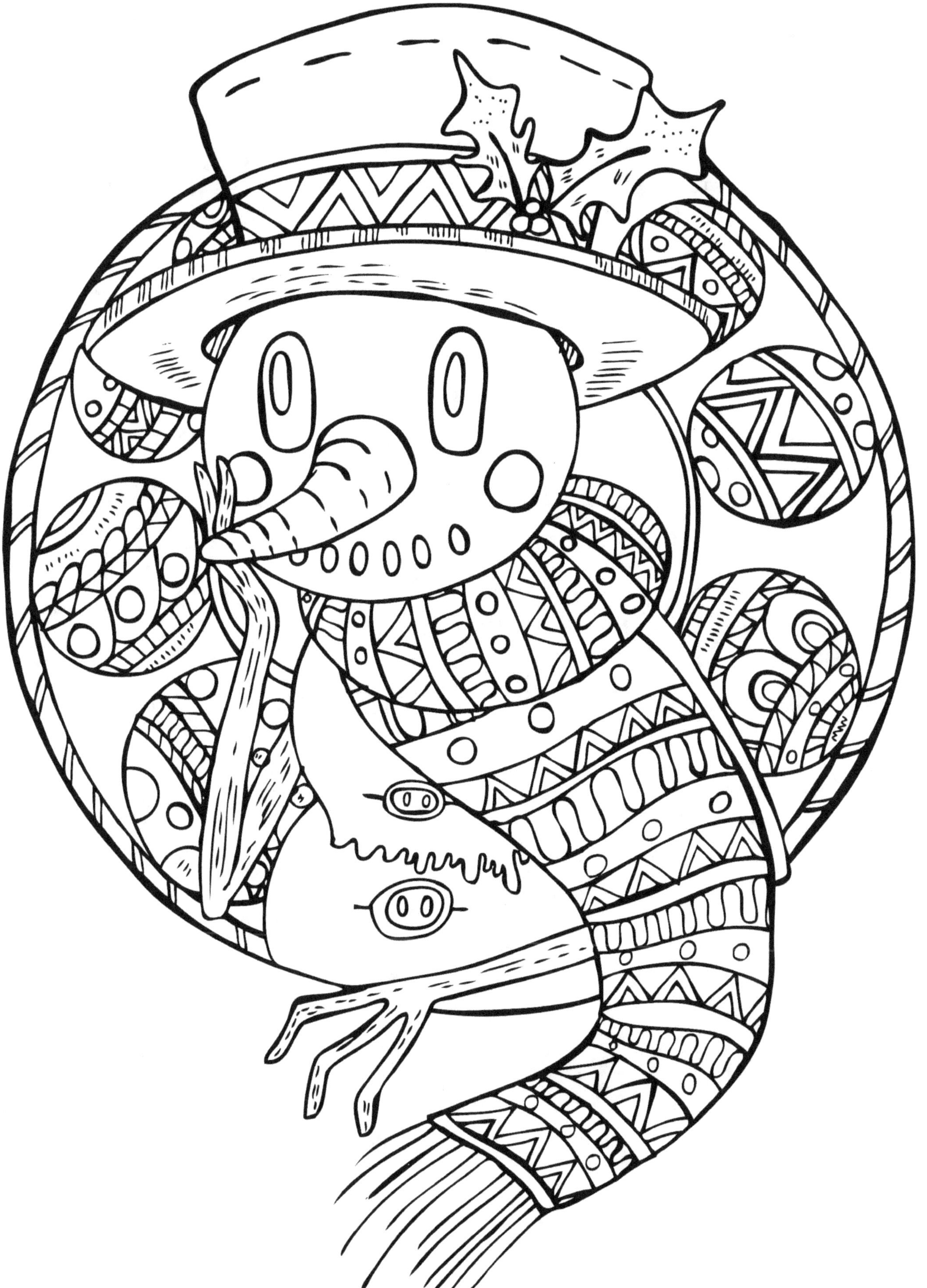

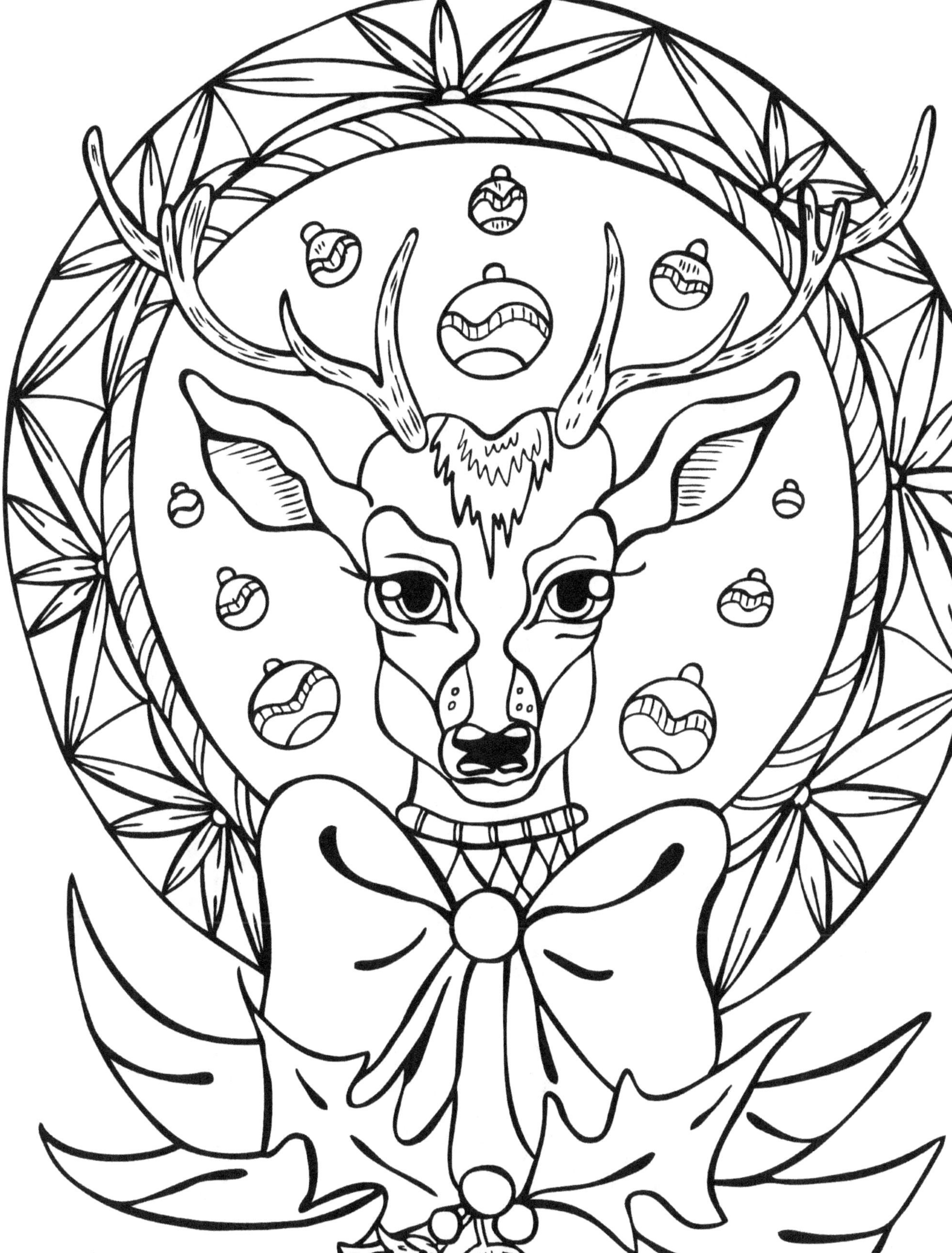

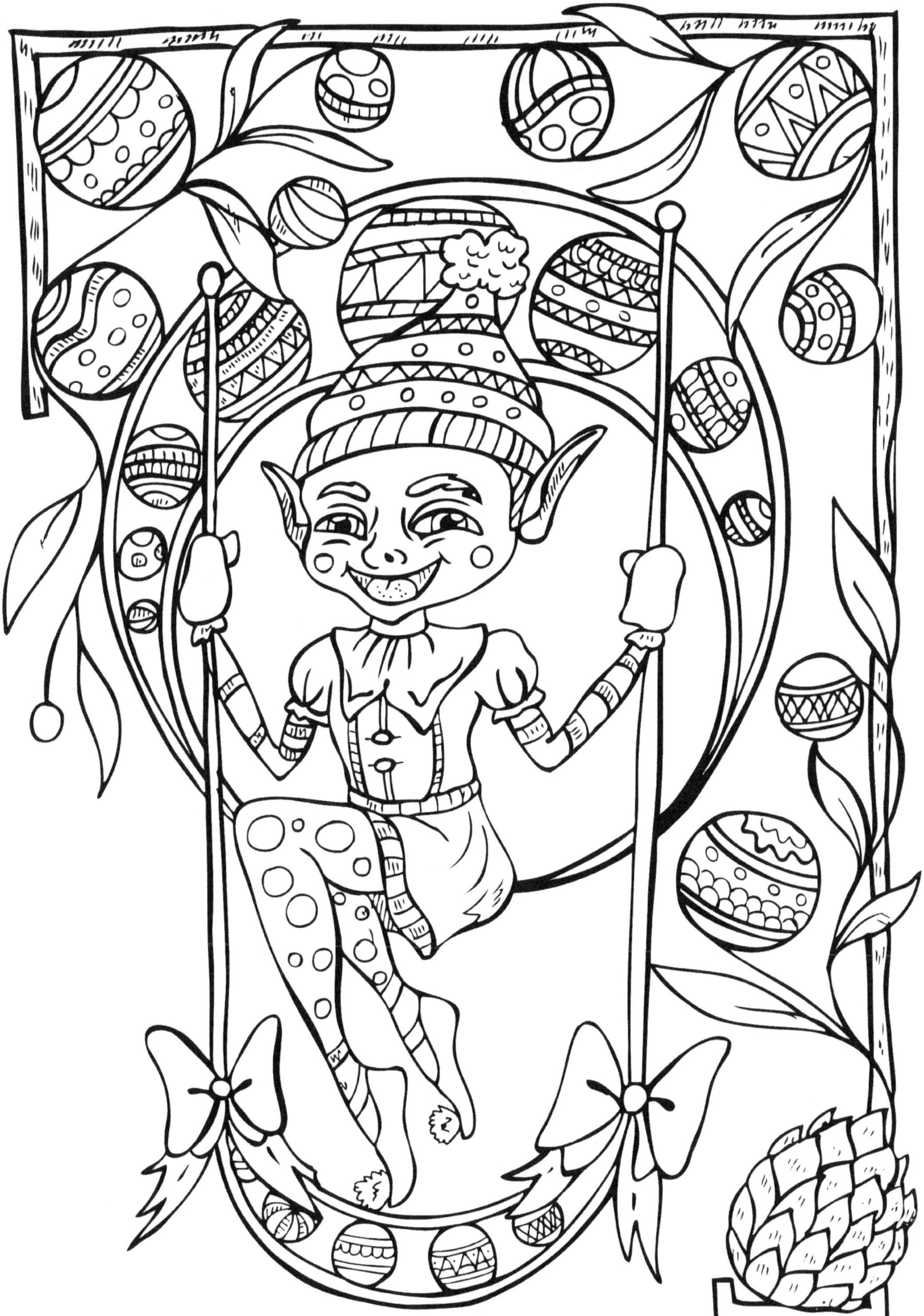

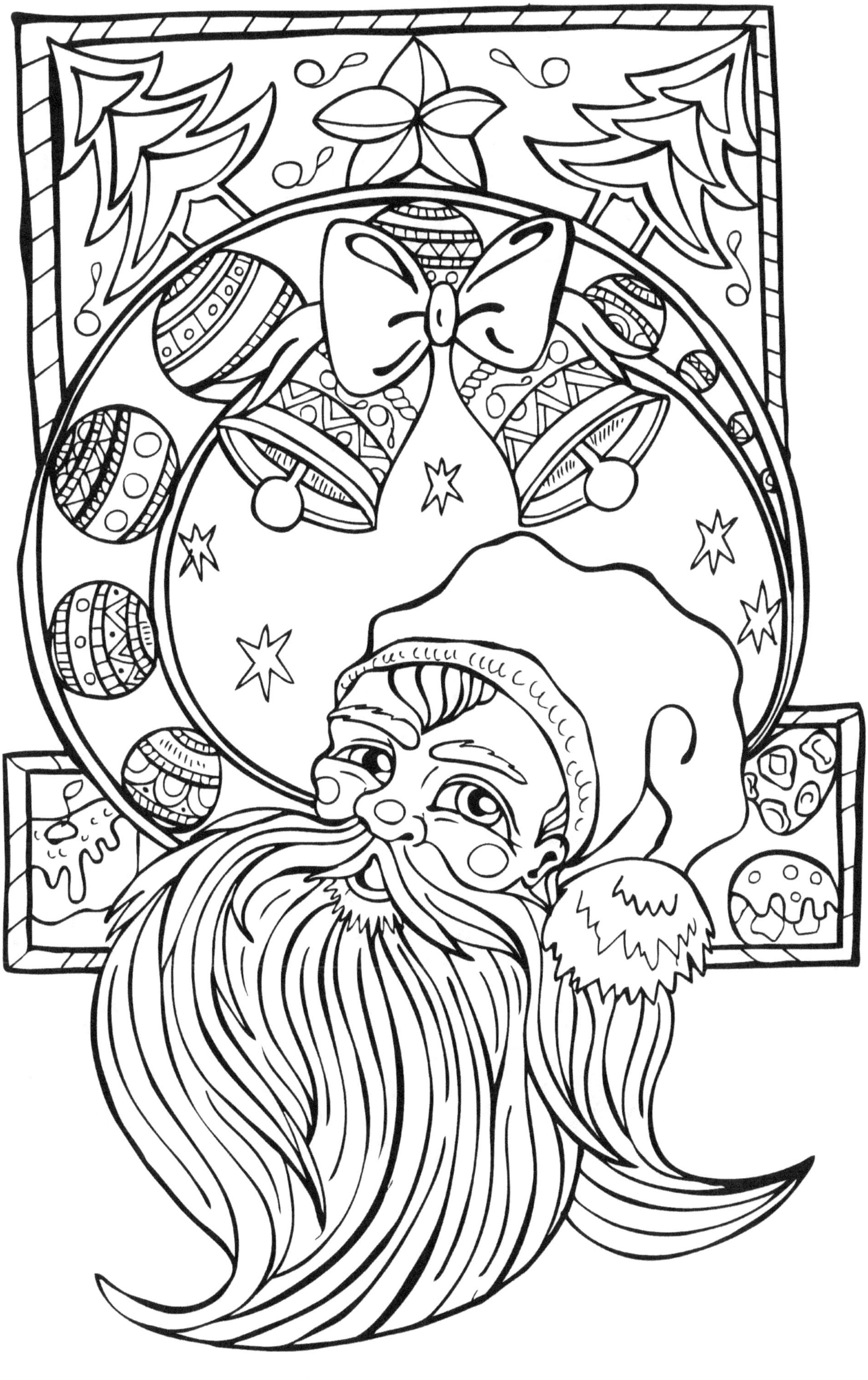

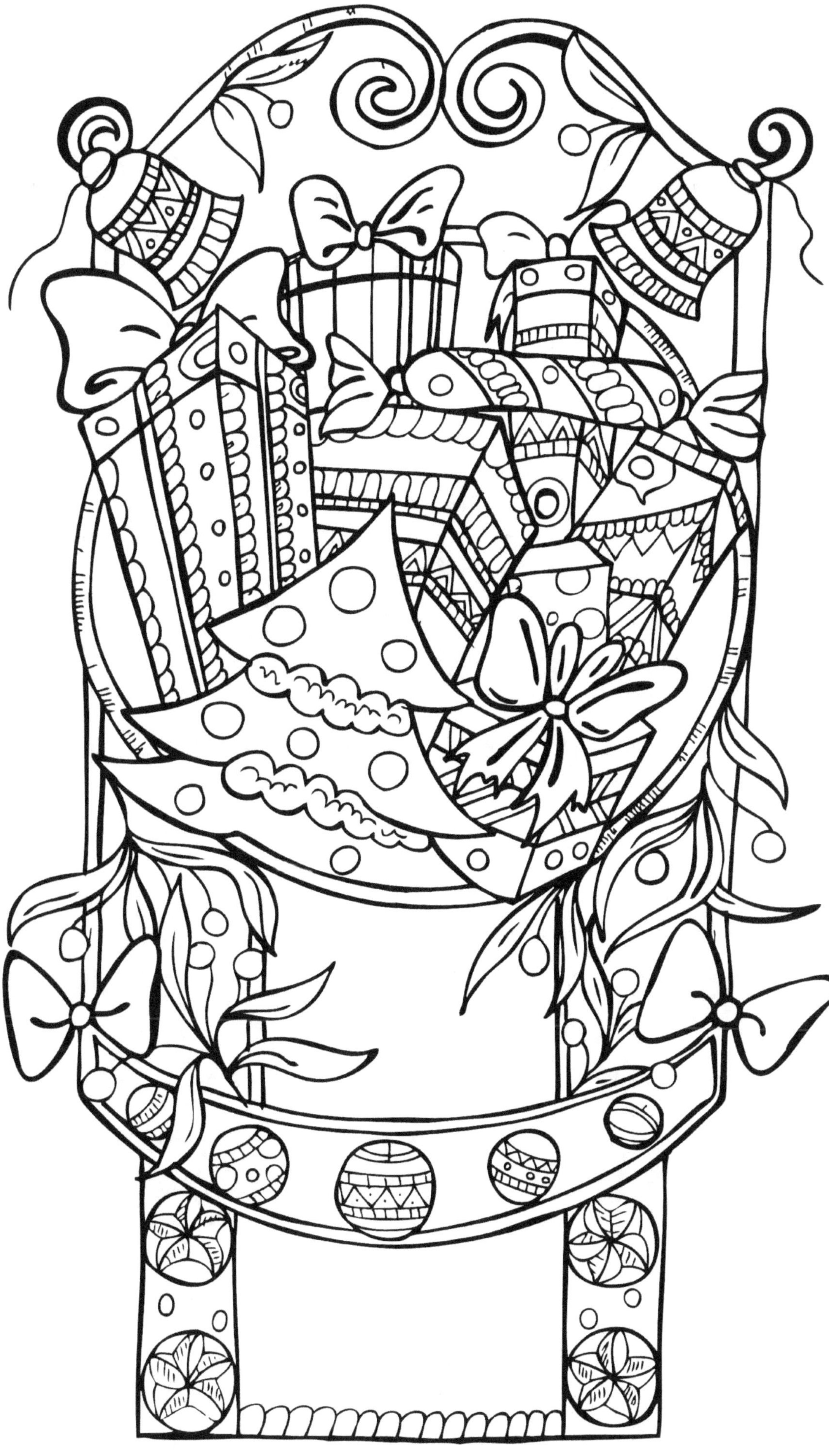

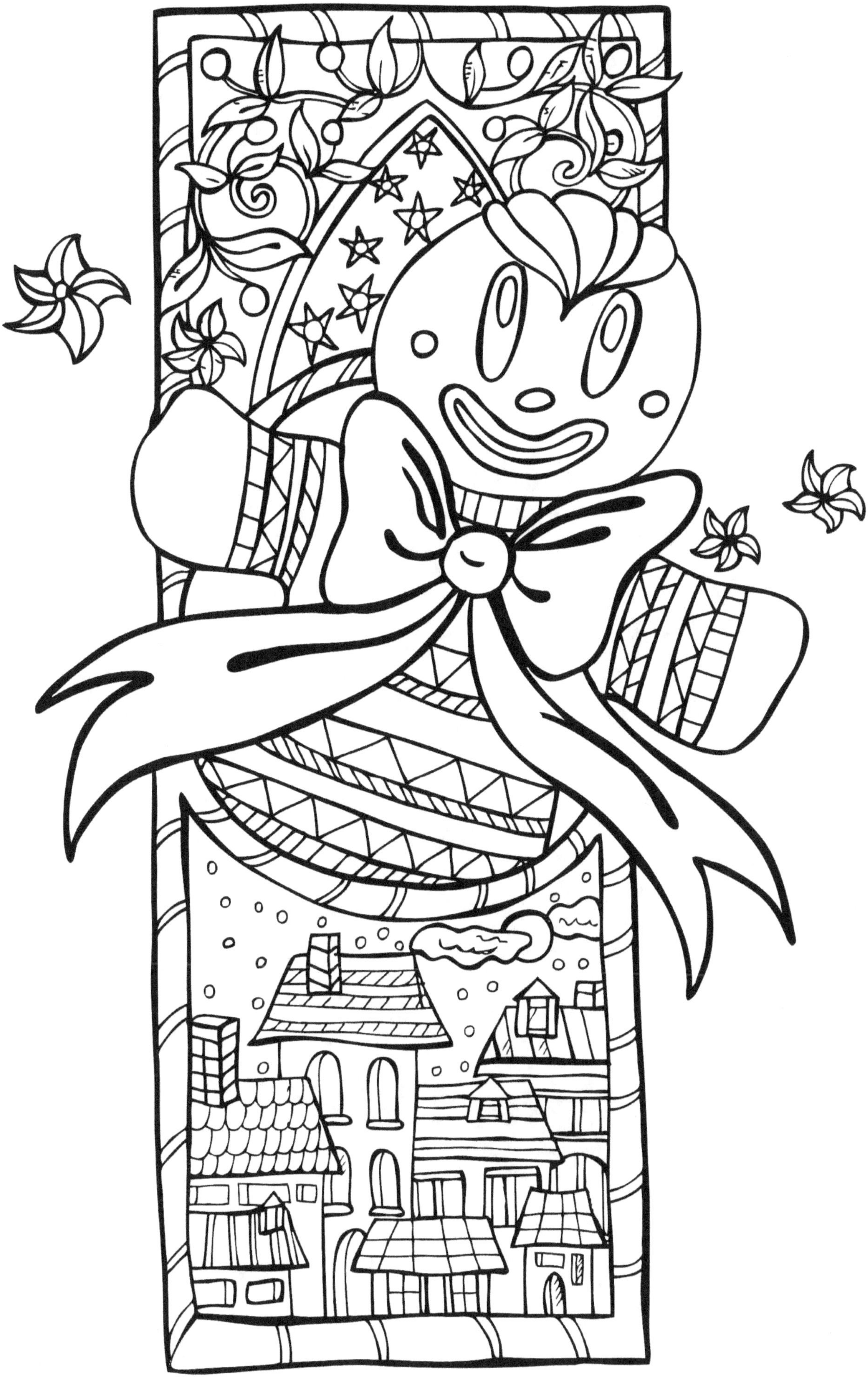

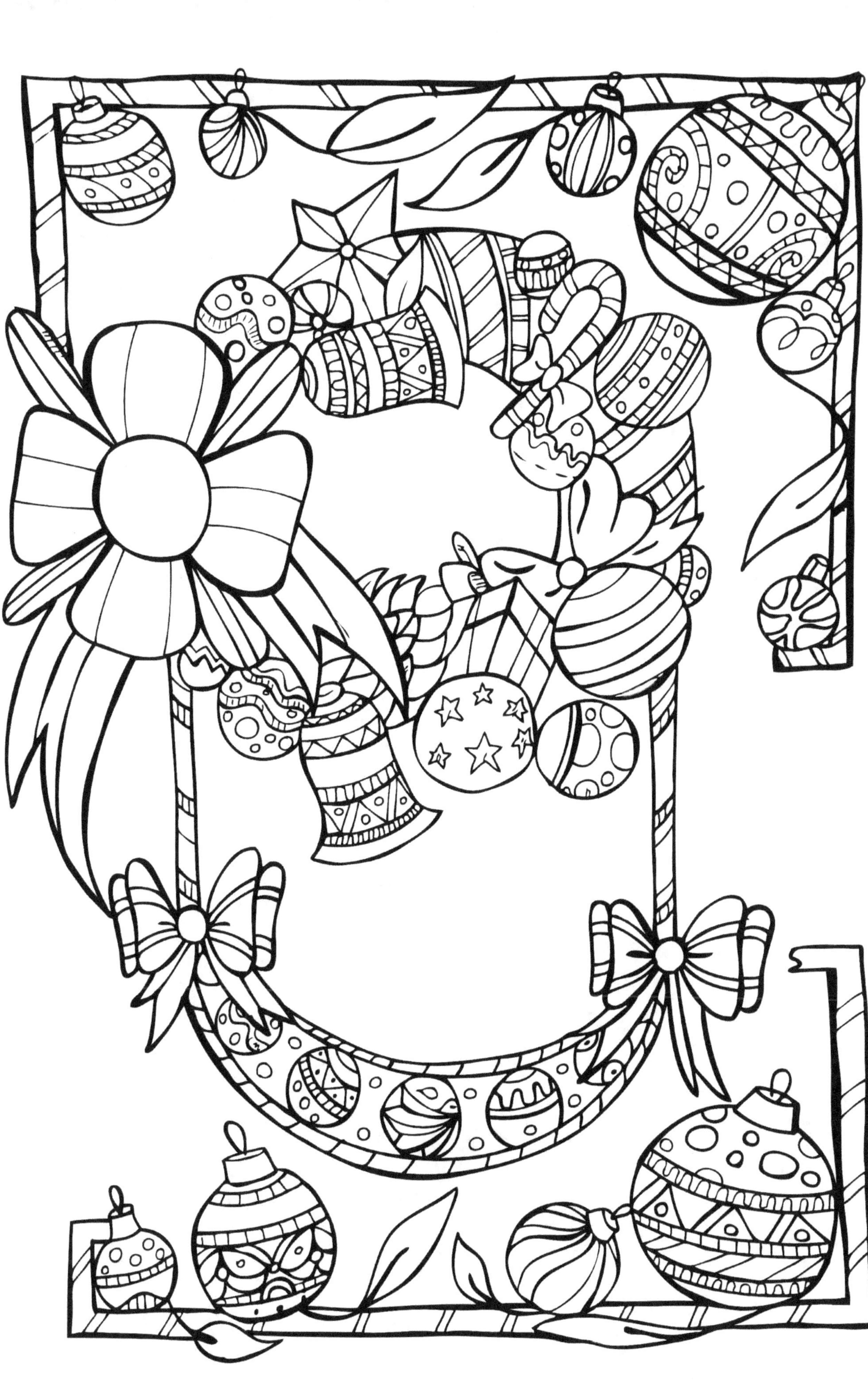

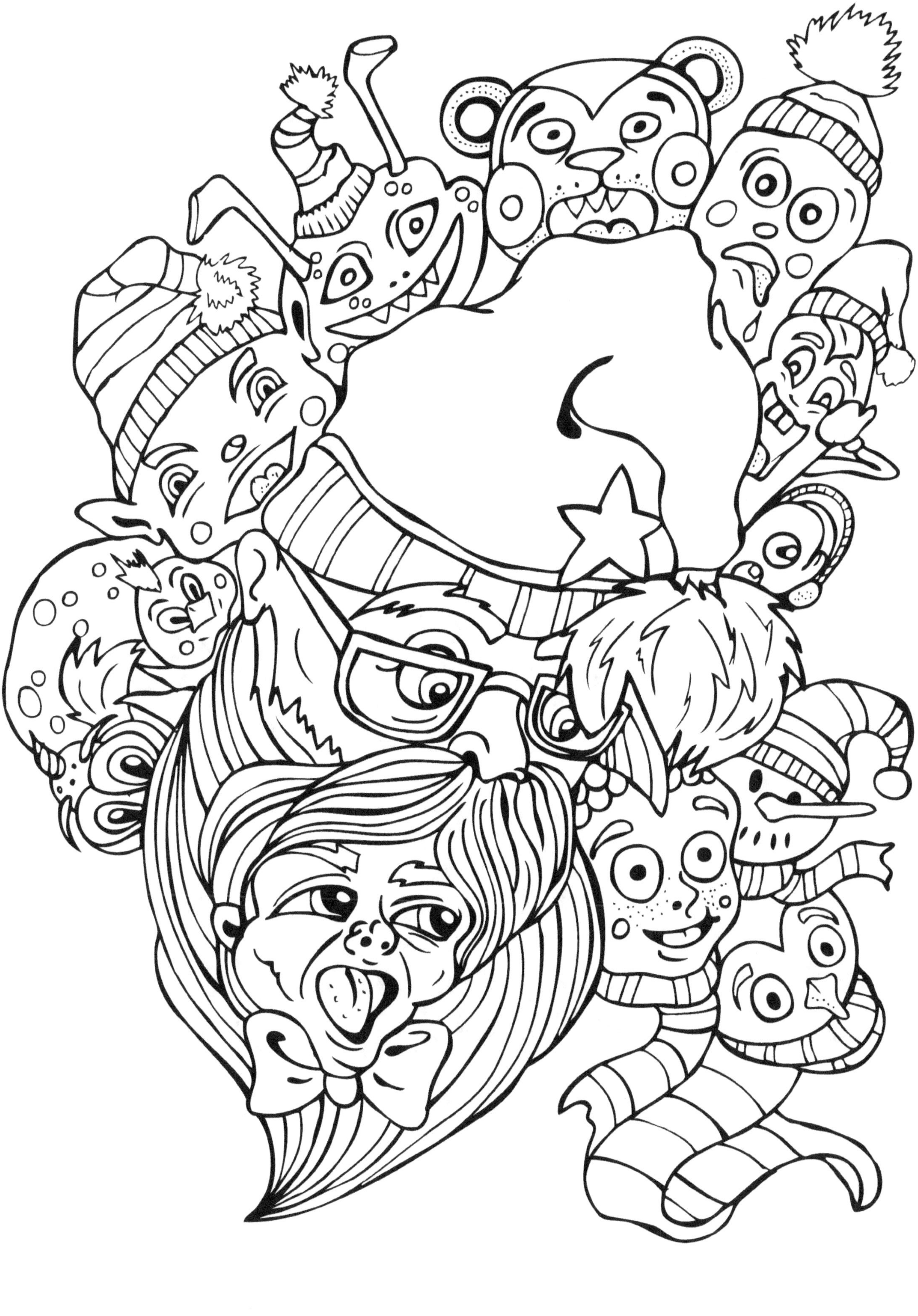

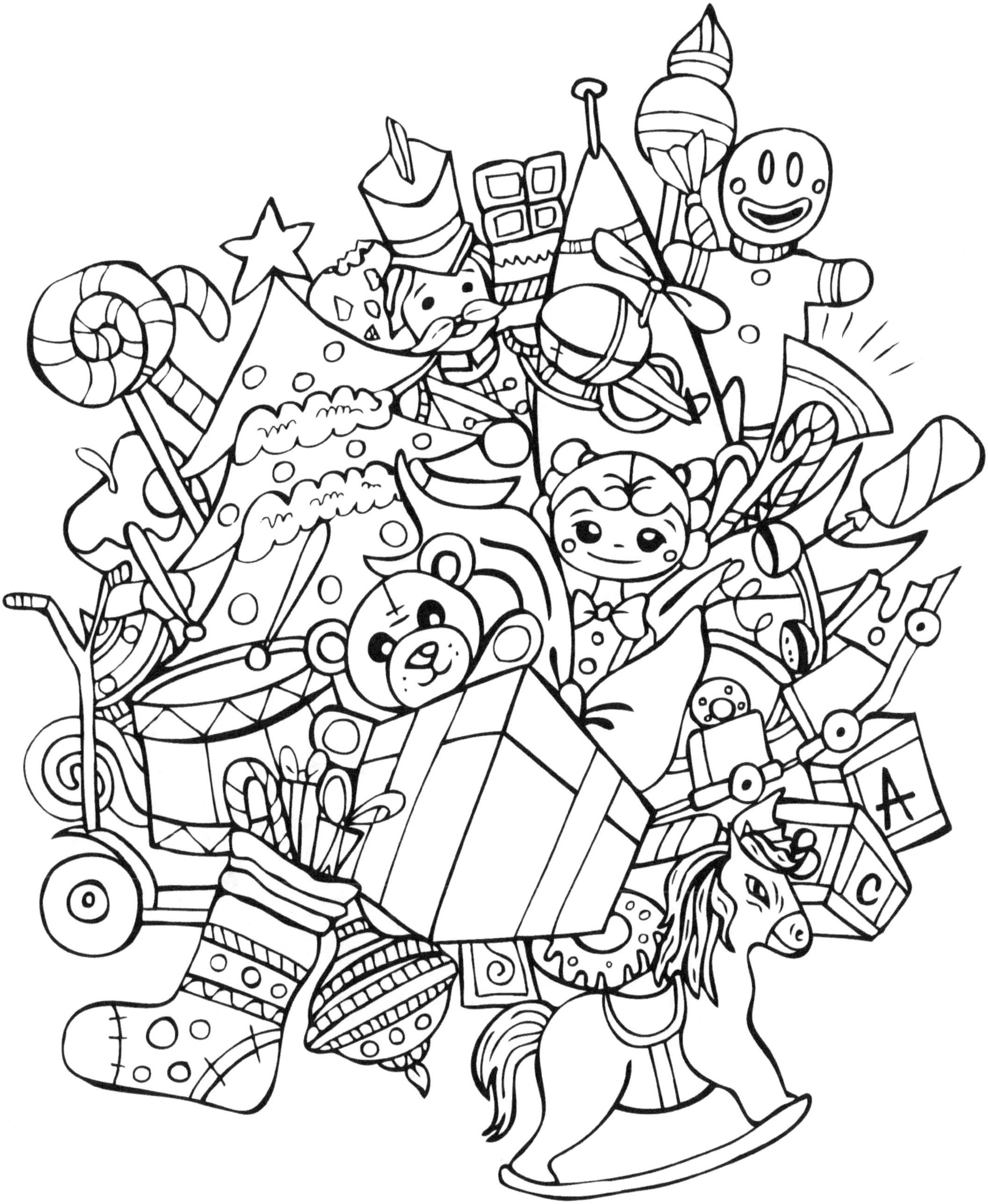
A
C

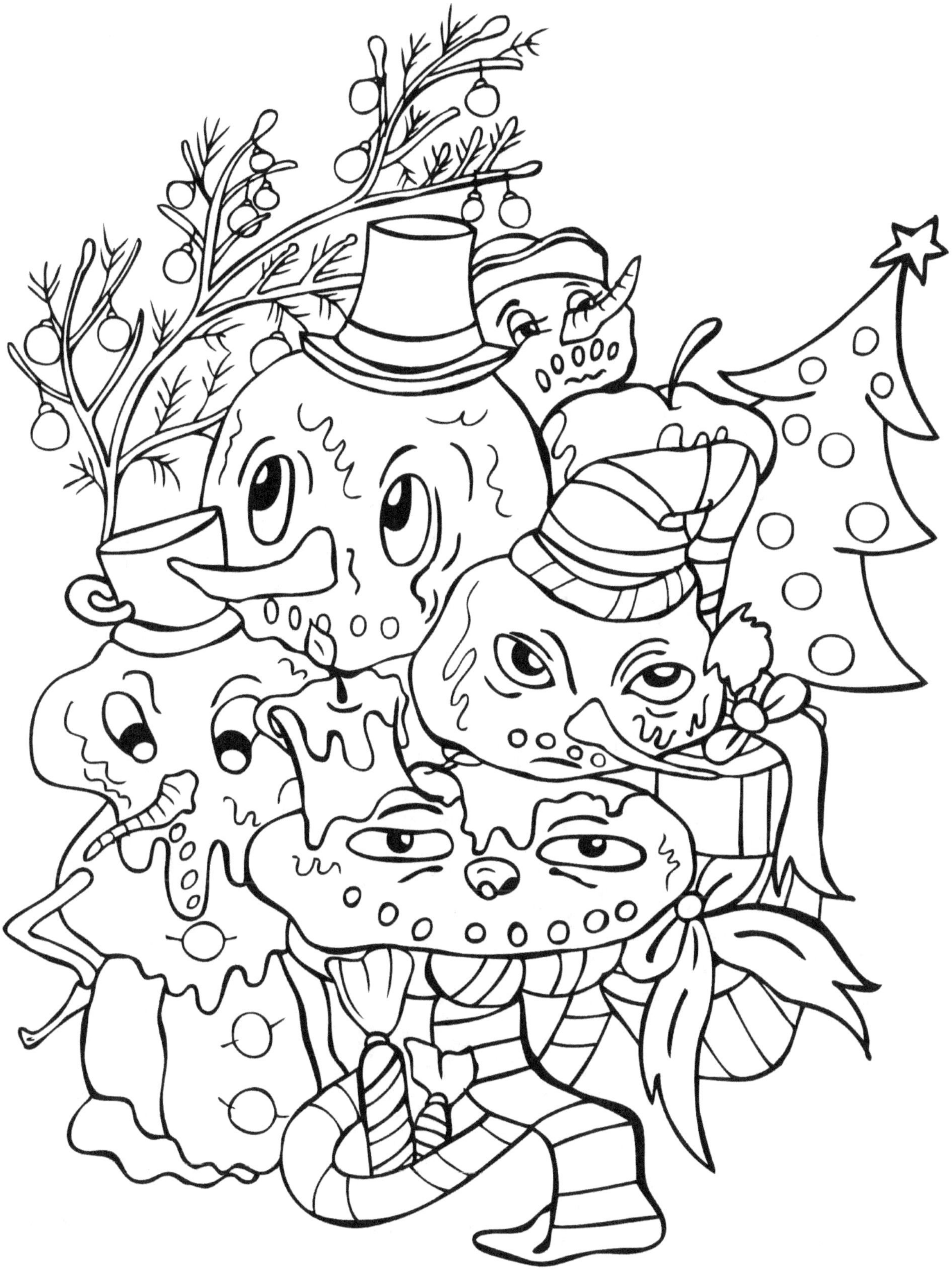

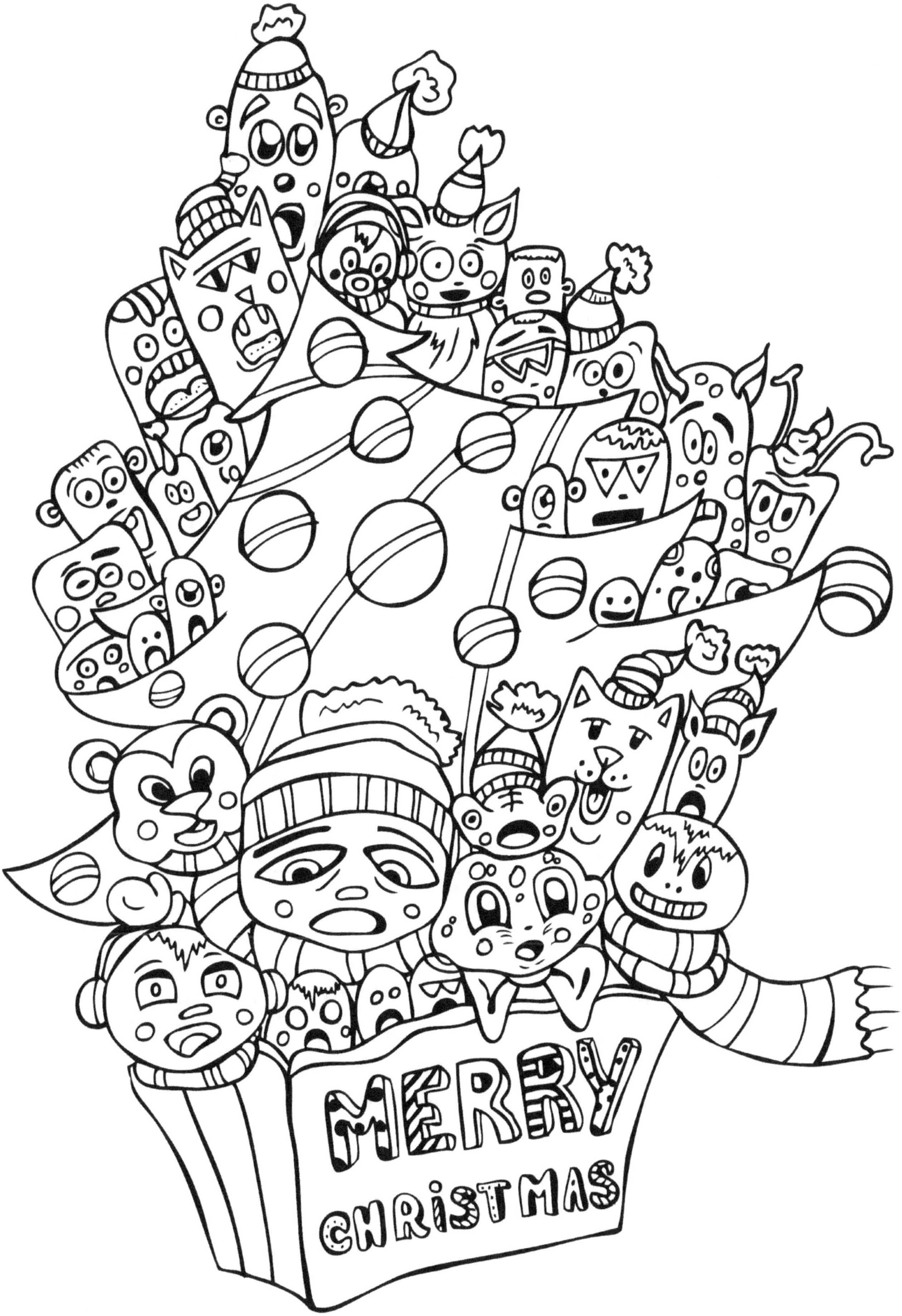
MERRY
CHRISTMAS

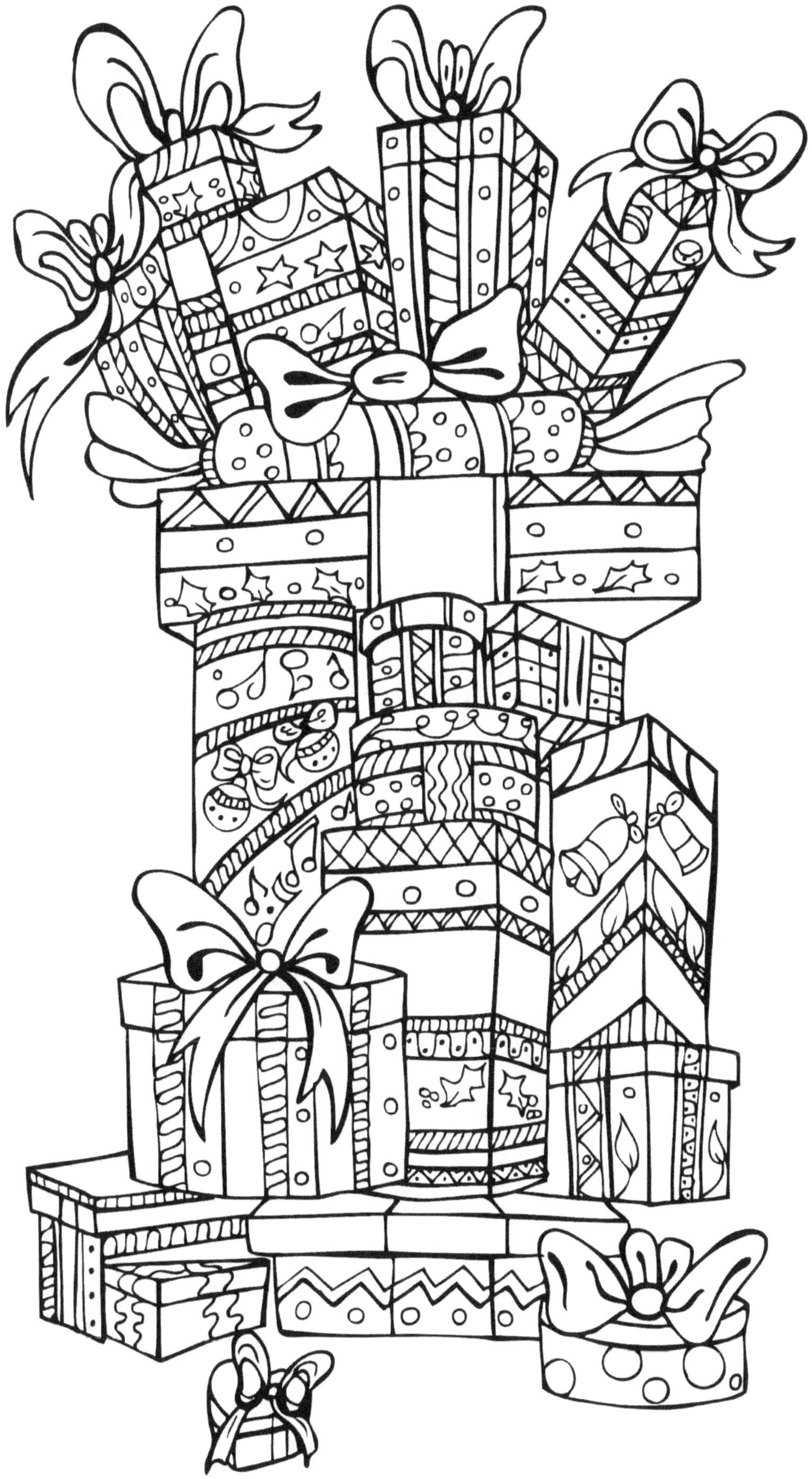

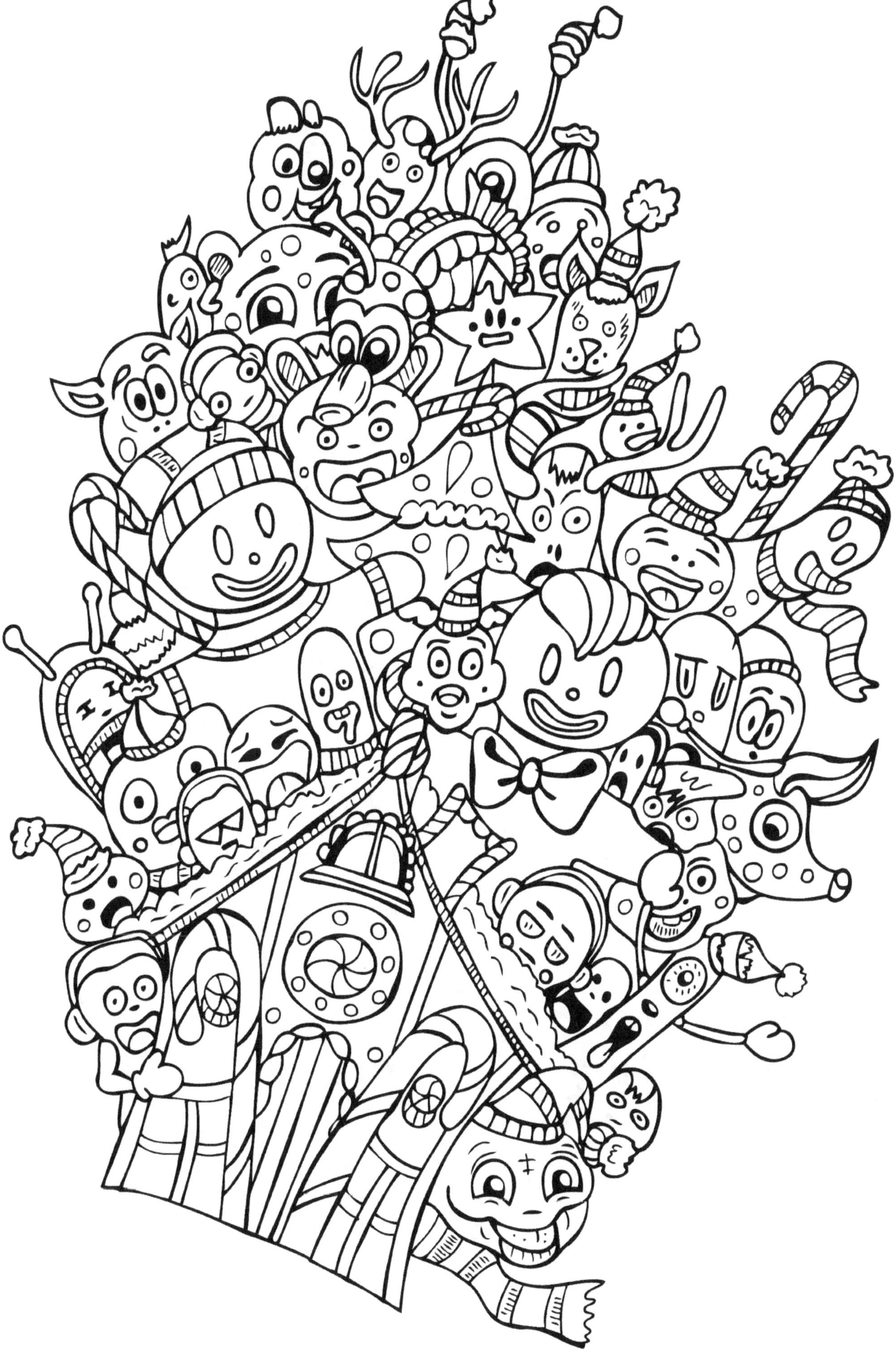

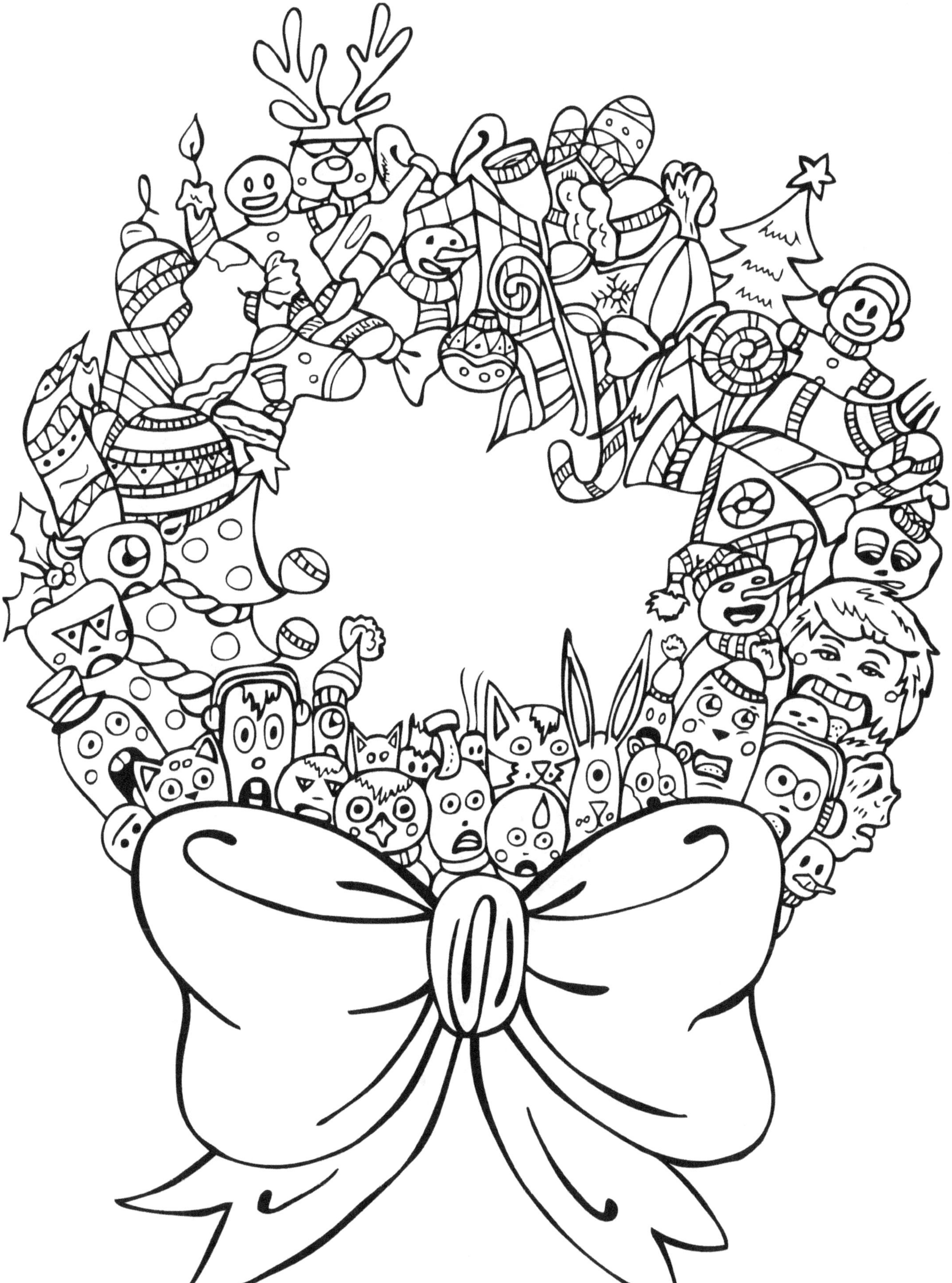

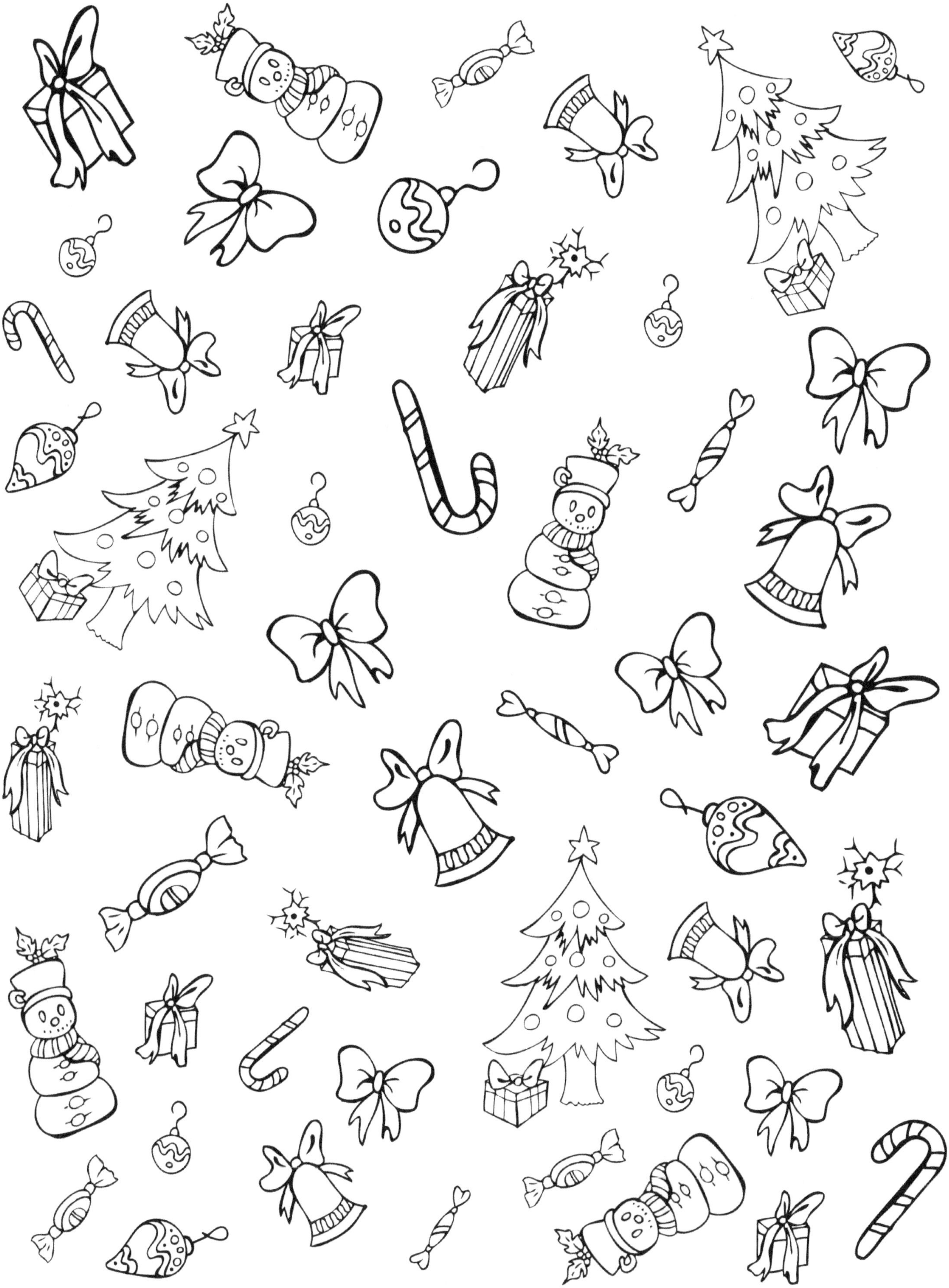

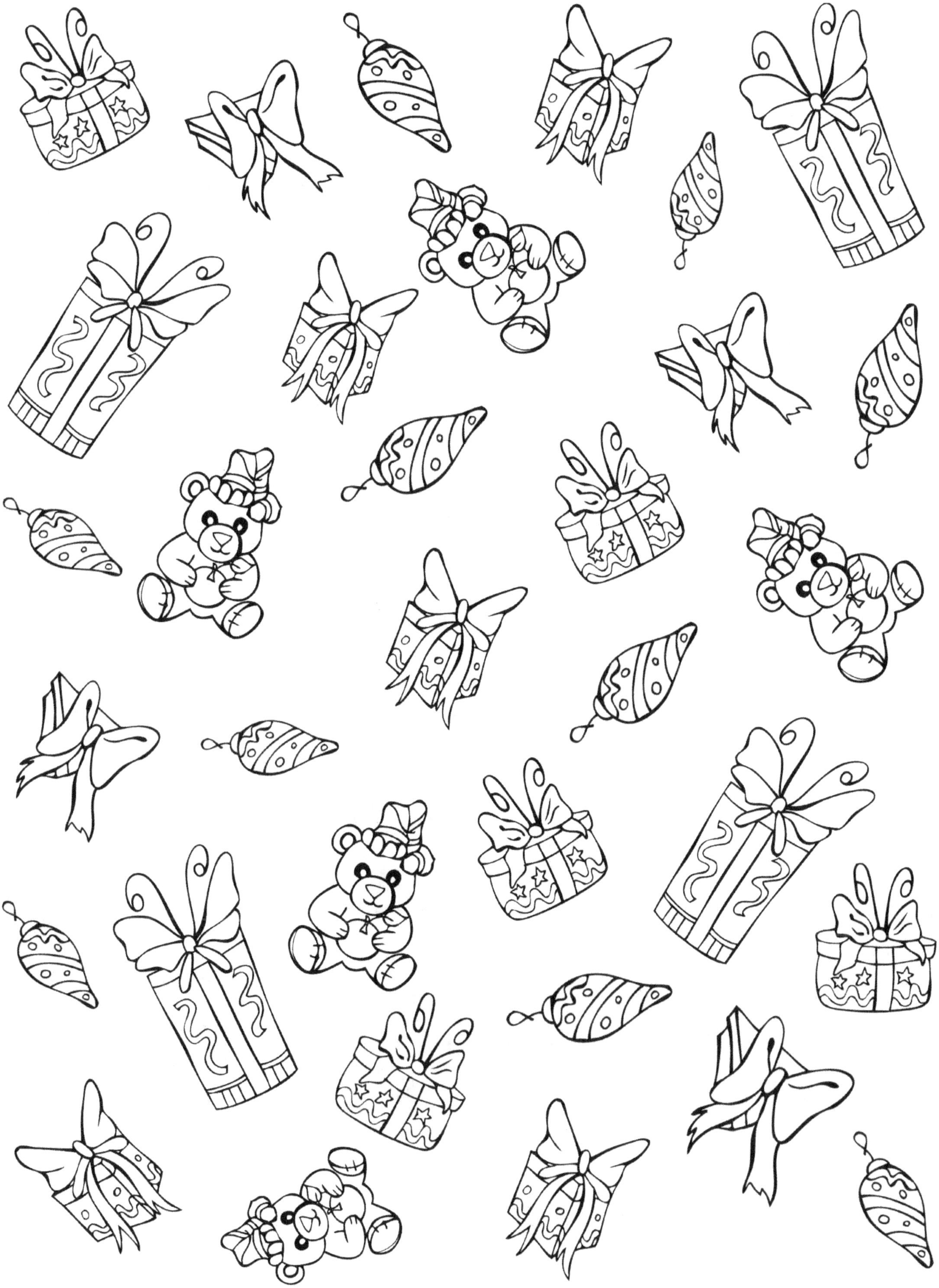

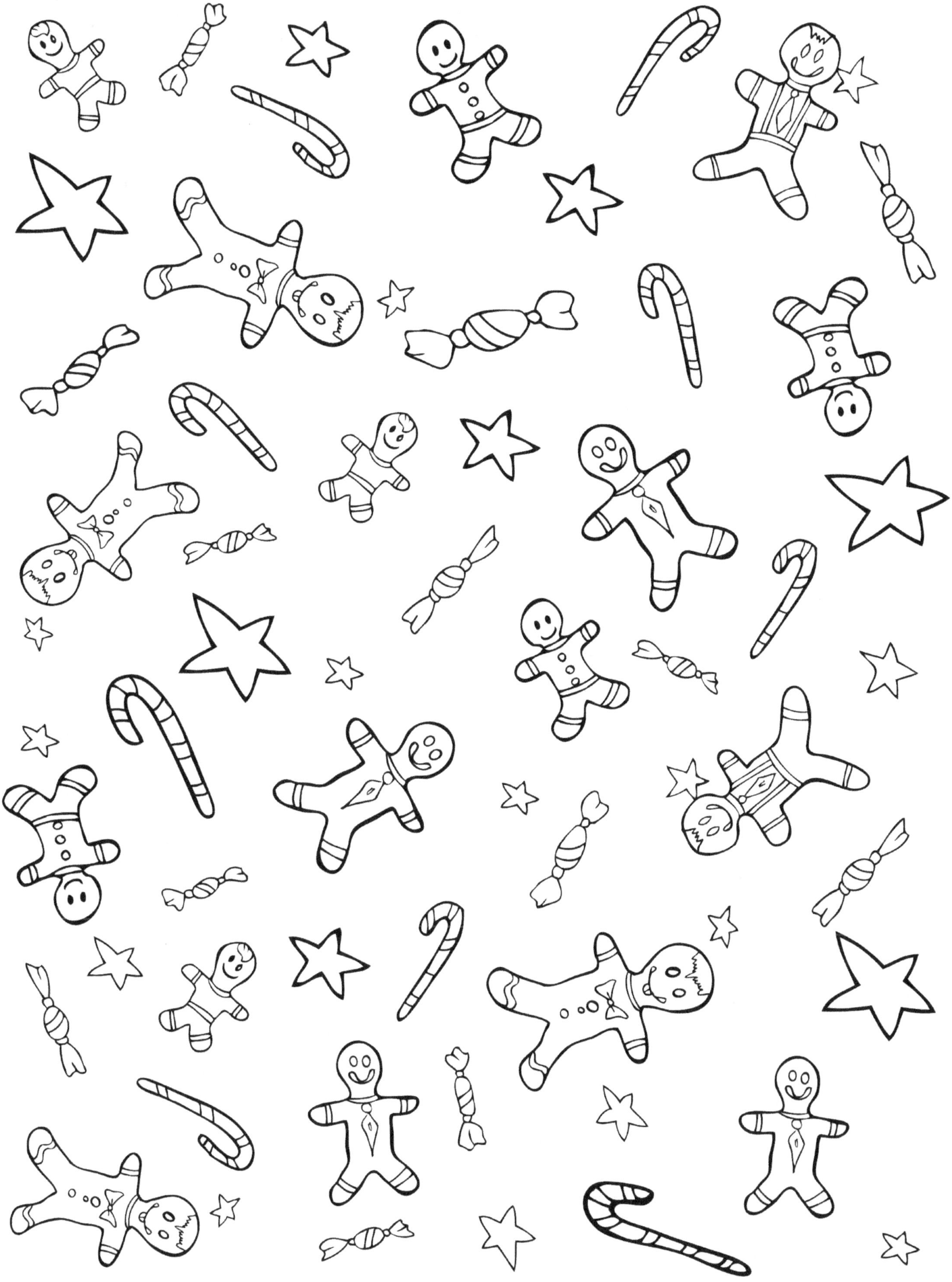

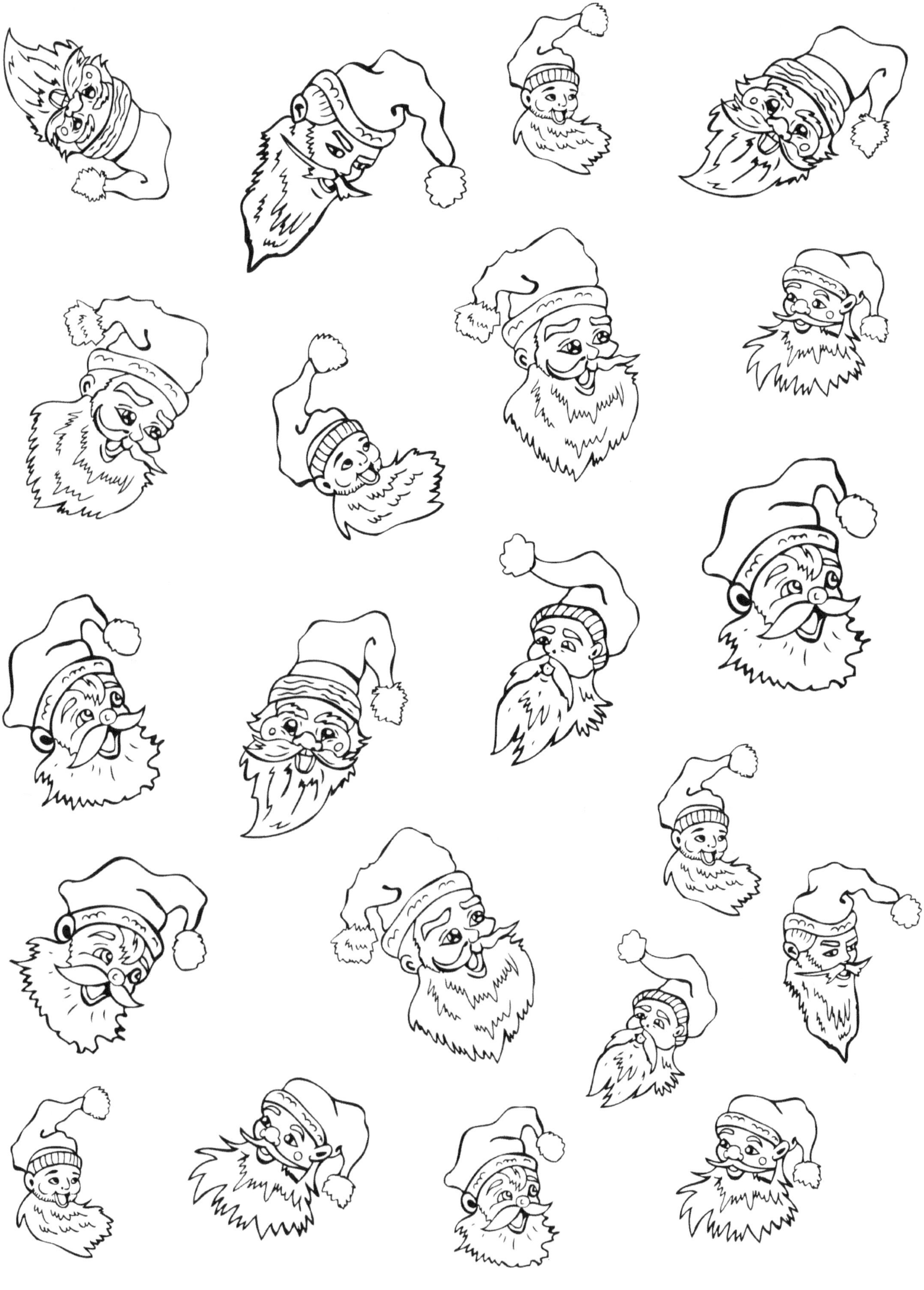

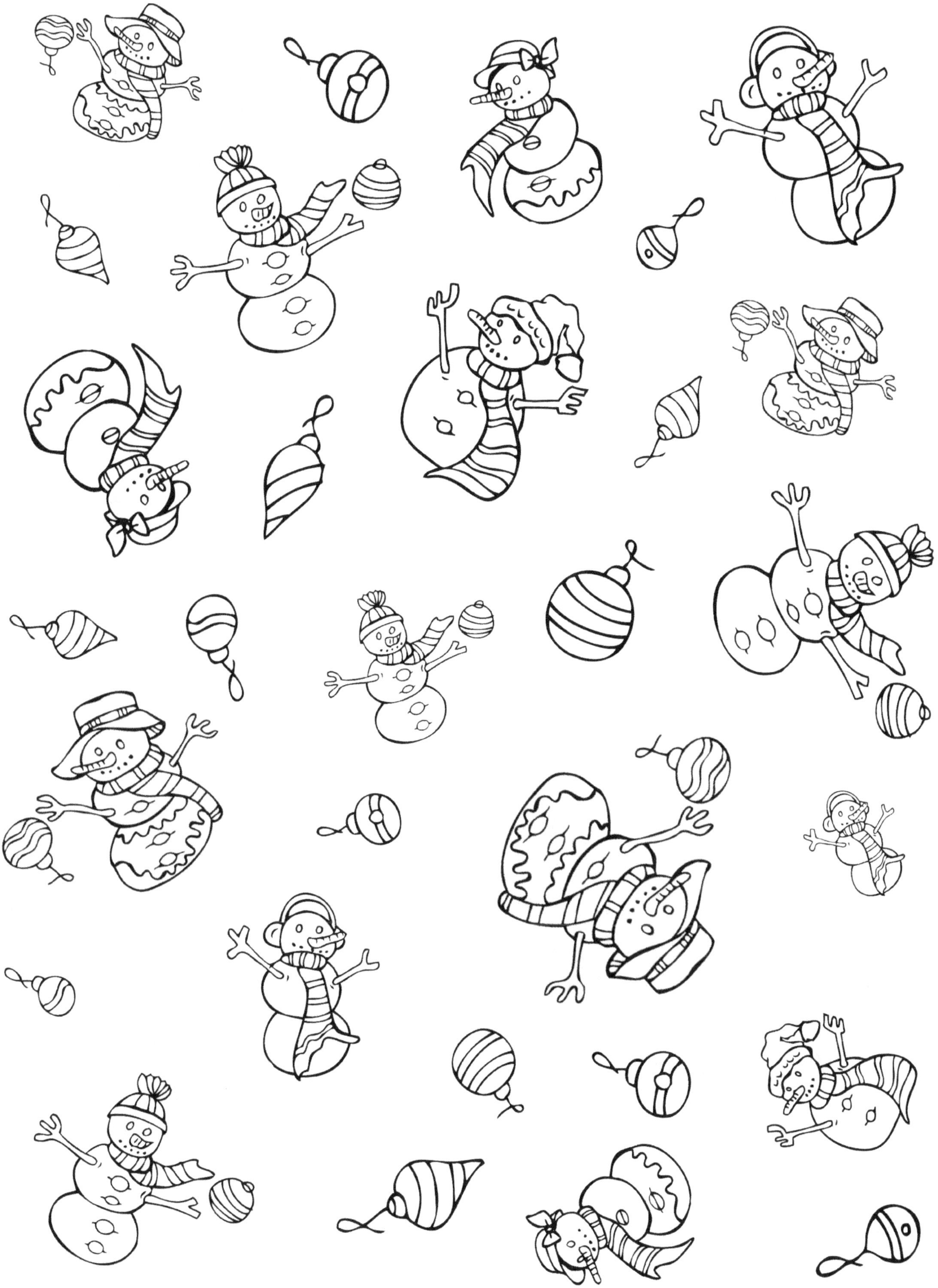

www.ingramcontent.com/pod-product-compliance
Lightning Source LLC
Chambersburg PA
CBHW081602170526
45166CB00009B/2798
* 9 7 8 1 5 2 2 8 0 8 0 4 6 *